The Hobby Book of Stenciling
and Brush-stroke Painting

Books by Raymond F. Yates

HOW TO RESTORE ANTIQUES

ANTIQUE FAKES AND THEIR DETECTION

ANTIQUE REPRODUCTIONS FOR THE HOME CRAFTSMAN

THE HOBBY BOOK OF STENCILING AND BRUSH-STROKE
PAINTING

In collaboration with Marguerite W. Yates:

A GUIDE TO VICTORIAN ANTIQUES

RAYMOND F. YATES

The Hobby Book of Stenciling
and Brush-stroke Painting

DRAWINGS AND MOST PHOTOGRAPHS BY THE AUTHOR

COLOR PHOTOGRAPHS BY DAVID E. MILLER

McGRAW-HILL BOOK COMPANY, INC.

NEW YORK   LONDON   TORONTO

TO HOWARD AND MILDRED BUDD

ACKNOWLEDGMENTS. The author wishes to acknowledge his indebtedness for assistance in the preparation of this volume to Mr. John Kent of the Historical Chart Company, and the Society for the Preservation of New England Antiquities; to The Essex Institute, Salem, Mass.; to Merriam and Sons, Hartford, Conn.; to the Metropolitan Museum of Art, New York City; to the Pennsylvania Historical Society; and to Miss Katharine Worden.

ACKNOWLEDGMENTS: The author wishes to acknowledge his indebtedness for assistance in the preparation of this volume to Mr. John Kenny of the Hitchcock Chair Company; to The Society for the Preservation of New England Antiquities; to The Essex Institute of Salem, Mass.; to M. Swift and Sons, Hartford, Conn.; to the Metropolitan Museum of Art, New York City; to the Pennsylvania Historical Society; and to Miss Katherine Worden.

CONTENTS

I. THE CRAFT OF STENCILING IN EARLY AMERICA, 1

II. COLOR AND OTHER MATERIALS, 13

III. COPYING AND CUTTING STENCILS, 18

IV. STENCIL MOTIFS, 28

V. STRIPPING AND RESTORING OLD FURNITURE, 35

VI. UNDERCOATINGS AND BACKGROUNDS, 41

VII. APPLYING STENCILS, 49

VIII. STRIPING, VARNISHING, AND ANTIQUING, 65

IX. PAINTING TIN TRAYS, 74

X. DECORATED TINWARE, 94

XI. PAINTING ON GLASS, 109

XII. PAINTING CLOCKFACES, 118

XIII. FRAKTUR, 126

INDEX, 129

CHAPTER I

The Craft of Stenciling in
Early America

THE STENCIL is one of the oldest decorative devices, so old indeed
that no amount of research would reveal the early genius who
devised it or the time of its first application. Some stenciled decorations still remain in ancient Buddhist temples, and not a few of
the very old cathedrals of Europe still provide evidence of its
employment many centuries ago. Therefore the wide use to which
the stencil was put in the decoration of furniture during the early
part of the nineteenth century amounted to revival rather than
invention.

Everything was hustle and bustle in the United States in 1825.
The progress of a young nation not yet on its economic feet had
been interrupted by an ill-advised war in 1812, and a feverish
effort to make amends and to correct a historical mistake was in
evidence. A network of canals and better roads was spreading out
over the Eastern and Middle Western sections of the country,
land speculation was rampant, population was growing rapidly,
and many would-be entrepreneurs were itching to satisfy growing
demands for better things and a better life.

The first inklings of the technological revolution that eventu-
ated in Detroit were in evidence. Two Englishmen, Henry Maudslay and Joseph Bramah, had brought the turning lathe to a higher
state of perfection; the steam-driven buzz saw made possible
faster lumbering and milling operations; Eli Whitney not only
showed the way to mass production of firearms with a musket
with interchangeable parts but also introduced the milling ma-

1

chine; and a then unknown tinker, Eli Terry, had shown the way to the mass market by mass-produced wooden clockworks.

The lone, independent craftsman working in his tiny shop with ancient skills and ancient hand tools was not suddenly replaced, but for the first time in history his position was being challenged. The next twenty-five years were to be years of change and revolution. Things had to be made more quickly and cheaply if markets were to be satisfied, and improvements came with sudden, devastating effects. The hand-guided tool alone was no longer sufficient. The carts, wagons, and pack-a-backs of the sharp Yankee peddlers began to carry bargains that people could not help purchasing—smartly patterned pressed glass from the factory at Sandwich, painted tinware, painted chairs, guaranteed clocks at one-third the usual price, squirrel guns that were to spell the doom of the Kentucky rifle makers, chinaware that was destined within the brief space of a few years to still forever the hand of the pewterer and to bring to an end his ancient and honorable craft, factory-woven and printed fabrics that eventually stopped the whir of the flax and wool wheels of the hinterlands.

It is against this background that the skill or craft of the early nineteenth-century decorative arts must be viewed. They were born of the urge for speed, and whatever they possessed in the way of "art" was in a measure accidental and wholly subservient to this demand for rapid duplication. We are dealing not with a lost art but with a practical application of American ingenuity to the needs of the time.

In these remarks, I do not intend to disparage or to minimize in the least the work of the old craftsmen and craftswomen. Some of it was clumsy and gaudy, and the skill required for it was largely in application rather than in design. The designs themselves were often crude and were limited by the cost of production. Yet the old stencils possess a charm today that can add much to our modern home decoration.

Stenciling has been called a form of folk art. No doubt it reflected in some measure the feeling and mood of the times, but above all it represented a commercial need. However, the important thing is that public interest in the craft has brought about its revival and a large number of people have a genuine regard for furniture so decorated and wish to be able to make such decorations themselves purely as a hobby. And stenciling does, indeed, offer alluring possibilities for a most satisfying hobby.

It may also be said of the craft that, in so far as it related to furniture, it had a certain artistic background as well as a commercial one. During the latter part of the eighteenth century, the brothers Adam in England, architects and furniture designers for the aristocracy, introduced the vogue for delicately painted furniture, much of it in mahogany and sandalwood and all of it in excellent taste. Only artists of high repute were engaged to decorate the pieces that were to reach the homes of the lords and dukes of England. Pergolesi, Cipriani, and Kauffmann were among the able artists employed. Especially popular among the exclusive Adam clients was the beautiful work of Angelica Kauffmann.

Naturally other late eighteenth-century makers and designers of cabinets (the Adam brothers never made furniture) attempted to capitalize on the market for painted furniture. Perhaps some of it reached America; at any rate the idea took hold here, and decorated furniture was produced for the carriage trade in this country during the latter part of the eighteenth century and as late as the 1840s. Here, too, it must have been considered very elegant and exclusive, although there were no Kauffmanns or Ciprianis to decorate it. It may also be said that the vogue was not so widespread as it was in England and France; painted furniture was not for the poor man, any more than the finer mahogany furniture that was being made at the time.

Nevertheless, if people of moderate means could not have mahogany, they could have pine that was made to look like mahogany. Some early and unsung genius of decoration produced what was called the "mahoganized" finish. When expertly done, the effect was excellent. Apparently the trick was turned by painting pine (a chest, for instance) with a sour-milk mixture of red and streaking it with lampblack or brown-black before the base coat dried. I have in my collection several items so finished, one of them a tall clock case of pine made about 1825. When carefully washed with soap and rubbed up and waxed, this "poor-man's mahogany" is delightfully quaint. This finish was also employed to some extent on so-called "fancy chairs."

The creation of imitation mahogany was followed by imitations of the elegant decorated furniture of the day. For this purpose, the stencil appeared to be the ideal means of cheap and rapid duplication. This method was relatively crude and awkward and had its limitations, but it had to do. That stenciling turned out to be a fairly flexible means of decoration argues well for the ingenuity of those early nineteenth-century artisans who learned how to use it so effectively.

The employment of the stencil as a means of decoration was not entirely new at the time the fancy chair was introduced in 1815 or slightly earlier. Once before, it had been employed as a substitute for much more expensive things—carpets, rugs, the expensive mural wallpapers, and other types of hand-printed papers that were imported from France before and after the American Revolution. Apparently, painted floors with stencil-produced designs and frescoed walls created by the same means were common in the 1760s. Indeed, such substitutes for luxuries were used in rural sections of the country up to the 1830s. I have seen examples of such work on the walls and floors of western New York farmhouses known to have been constructed during the 1820s and late 1830s. After that, the craft expired because of the availability of rugs and wallpaper to people who were growing wealthier. In one such home, still lived in by surviving members of the family who built it, the itinerant artist (if artist he could be called) remained with the family for the whole winter while he applied his craft to the bare plaster.

While countless thousands of fancy chairs with stenciled decorations began to appear in the 1820s, this was not the only article of American furniture that was so treated. Undoubtedly it was the

Fig. 1. Early fancy chair, which is considerably less elaborate than those that followed in the late 1820s and early 1830s. (*Courtesy of Essex Institute, Salem, Mass.*)

Fig. 2. Stencil decoration was applied to every form of furniture during the 1820s and 1830s. This typical late American Empire piano was made in New York by George Tallmann. The fruit motif designs in the upper panels represent the largest form of stencil patterns ever used. (*Courtesy of the Metropolitan Museum of Art.*)

Fig. 3. Stenciled headboard of a late American Empire four-poster bed made about 1825. The Masonic motif noted was not unusual on clocks but rarely appeared on other furniture.

chair that set the fashion, but several other articles of furniture decorated in this manner appeared during the latter part of the American Empire period. One of my most cherished possessions is an Empire four-poster bed in maple with a stenciled headboard and a stenciled blanket roll at the foot—the blanket roll being a baluster running across the bottom that can be turned in sockets bored into the two posts. The decorations are Masonic in motif, in gold or bronze against a black background. Beds thus decorated are difficult to find; unlike chairs, they were not made by the hundreds of thousands.

Some Empire chests were also decorated with stencils, although during fifteen-odd years of searching out unusual antiques in various sections of the country, I have come upon only three of them. The fact that they existed, however, is worth mentioning for the benefit of those who wish to decorate an old chest; they may do so with the assurance that such decoration was authentic and "in period."

The same holds true for beds. Any bed of the period *could have been* so treated. As a matter of fact, it is difficult to think of a single item of furniture made from 1820 to 1840 that could not have been decorated, unless it was associated with Phyfe, Sheraton, Hepple-white, or Chippendale. The influence of all of these craftsmen, with the exception of Phyfe, lived on after them. One would not, for instance, care to plaster with stencils a Pembroke table or a table whose maker was consciously or unconsciously influenced by Hepplewhite or Chippendale. So far as I know, no such pieces ever appeared, with the possible exception of certain fancy chairs that owed something to the Sheraton influence.

Anyone who has spent any time at all in antique shops has come upon examples—and fine ones, too—of the early wooden-works and brass-works shelf-clock cases that were stencil-dec-orated. Not only were the cornices and pilasters of these clocks so decorated, but the borders of the glasses as well, the latter usually in gold leaf.

The Empire mirror, like the clock, often bore stencils; always, indeed, when it did not boast of a mahogany frame with carving. Invariably frames so decorated were of cheap wood, often pine, covered with a first coat of gesso.

Here and there, but still as scarce as hen's teeth, a stenciled bedside table turns up. And of course there is the fancy stenciled bench, and the Windsor or Boston rocker, which may have been the first type of chair so treated. The dates of the early part of this business have never been firmly set. No one knows precisely when the first fancy chair appeared or whether it preceded or followed the first fancy Boston rocker.

That the name of Lambert Hitchcock has become so firmly riveted to the fancy chair is somewhat of a mystery. Clearly he was not the first to make it, nor the last; the business, in a degraded state, lasted into the late 1860s, long after Hitchcock's death. It was not until 1818, a number of years after painted chairs had been introduced, that Hitchcock started his business in Con-necticut. The exact time of the appearance of the first ones is not definitely known. Various guesses have been made, one perhaps as good as another. It would seem that such chairs first appeared in small numbers during the very early part of the nineteenth cen-

Fig. 4. Pre-Hitchcock painted fancy chairs from the famous Captain Crowninshield's *Cleopatra's Barge*. The chairs date from about 1817. (*Courtesy of Essex Institute, Salem, Mass.*)

tury. There is some historical evidence from the year 1817 that may be used to confirm their appearance. It was during that year that the fabulous sailing yacht *Cleopatra's Barge* was launched at Salem, Massachusetts, and began its world tour under the direction of its captain and owner, George Crowninshield. Some of the furnishings of this yacht are preserved in museums and private collections. Included are a number of Salem-made fancy chairs of the Sheraton type.

In attempting to piece together the history of fancy chairs and other stenciled articles, it might be advisable to place the eighteenth-century lacquered pieces in the historical background. During the eighteenth century many American-produced highboys in a raw state of finish were loaded on sailing vessels and taken to China, where they were decorated with lacquer and gold. Then there was the story of Louis XV's coach painter, Martin, and his wonderful invention of colored enamels that became known in France as *vernis-Martin*.

Thus investigation brings forth the fact that the fancy chair and other stenciled furniture did not result from any sudden inspiration but were rather a natural end product of an evolutionary trend. Certainly it is difficult to credit any one person for the craft of decorating furniture by means of stencils.

That Lambert Hitchcock did not introduce the fancy chair is proved by advertisements of such articles in the New York City Directory as early as 1810, eight years before the enterprising young Hitchcock set up his first chair factory in the tiny Connecticut hamlet of Barkhamsted. For a number of years his chairs were sold only in bundled kits for assembly and finishing in the Southern market to which practically all of his products were shipped. His success in this venture was so great and his employees were so numerous (for that time) that a small community was established, with his factory as its nucleus. This was named Hitchcockville.

In 1826, Hitchcock, in an effort to keep abreast of his rapidly growing business, occupied a "modern" brick building. By this time he had abandoned the merchandising of his kit of chair parts and was making complete chairs with stenciled decorations. His products also began to include Windsor or Boston rockers and the so-called "Cape Cod benches," or rocking settees.

Although Hitchcock cannot be credited with being the originator of the fancy chair, it is certain that his chair designs and construction established standards that were well worth copying. Indeed, they were copied so faithfully that unless such chairs bore his stenciled trade-mark on the rear edge of the seat (L. Hitchcock Hitchcockville, Conn., Warranted) it was—and still is—difficult to set them apart from other products of the time.

Fig. 5. Lambert Hitchcock's factory at Hitchcockville, Conn., now Riverton. At the time of its construction, it was the largest chair manufactory in
the United States. The Hitchcock Chair Company has been revived and now
produces fancy chairs in the manner of and with the methods employed by
the original owner 125 years ago.

Even before his new plant was opened at Hitchcockville, Lambert had hundreds of small competitors. In the parade in New
York City that celebrated the opening of the Erie Canal in 1825,
some two hundred members of the Chair-Makers Society marched,
proudly carrying their banner with a chair on it and the slogan
"Rest for the Weary."

It is interesting to note that Lambert Hitchcock's old Hitchcockville factory (now Riverton, Connecticut) is again producing
Hitchcock fancy chairs just as America's most famous early chair-
maker produced them while John Quincy Adams was President of
the United States. It all came about quite accidentally when a
young Hartford, Connecticut, businessman, Jack Kenny, spent a
fruitless morning casting in the Framingham River, which runs
hard by the quaint old factory that Lambert built with pride and

Fig. 6. A Chair-Makers Society banner carried in the New York City Parade that celebrated the opening of the Grand Erie Canal in 1825. During the 1840s there were some 6,000 small and large chairmakers in the U.S.A.

joy in 1826. Disgusted with his luck, young Mr. Kenny was attracted to the old building and investigated its windowless hulk. The basement was filled with river-borne silt from spring floods, the floors creaked menacingly when walked upon, and the roof was little more than a sieve. Yet Kenny sensed the spirit of the place and decided to reestablish the businesss that had . once flourished there.

After several years of patient searching for the production details of the original Hitchcock chairs and the expenditure of some $70,000 in the rehabilitation of the factory, Jack Kenny with two associates, Richard Coombs, a former house contractor, and Kenneth Frazee, a World War II bomber pilot, brought Lambert Hitchcock into fair and profitable competition with Grand Rapids. After a lapse of more than one hundred years, Hitchcock is back in business at the exact point and with the exact methods used

Fig. 7. Expert striping fancy chairs at the factory of the Hitchcock Chair Company, Riverton, Conn. Like Hitchcock's chairs of old, the new ones are made of native rock maple with seats of rush harvested in nearby swamps.

when he abandoned his enterprise. The modern Hitchcock chair is not a reproduction but a revival. It is made of the same sturdy rock maple as of old, and the rush for its seat is gathered from the same swamps where Hitchcock's employees waded through the water and mud to cut and bundle it. The stenciling, too, is so skillfully done that no apologies to original work are in order. And just as Lambert Hitchcock worried about meeting the demands of 1826, Messrs. Kenny, Coombs, and Frazee are worrying about meeting the consumer demands of today.

CHAPTER II

Color and Other Materials

THE MATERIALS needed for decorative work of the sort described in this book are neither numerous nor costly. With the expenditure of a few dollars the beginner may produce a large number of pieces before a replenishment of materials is required.

The small stock of brushes should be of the finest quality. The cost difference between a good brush and a poor one is so small that there is little excuse for the purchase of the latter. Some of these brushes will be required for use with varnish, and varnish will pull bristles from a brush when they are not firmly anchored. Five-cent brushes of the sort school children use for water-color painting are not suitable.

We should have at least a half-dozen camel's-hair brushes of the type used for professional water-color work, ranging in size from small to large. They can be purchased in any well-stocked paint store.

For wide coverage with varnish we shall need a brush 1½ inches wide, of the finest possible quality. Let us by all means shun the twenty-five-cent variety.

We should also have in our brush kit three quill brushes, ½-, ¾-, and 1-inch sizes. To complete the list, we add a 1½-inch striping brush and, for wider lines, a ⅜-inch striping brush.

Other materials needed are listed below:

1 quart turpentine
1 pint Valspar 24-hour varnish
1 pint Super-Valspar

1 pint flat black paint for backgrounds

1 roll masking tape

1 tube each of the following artist's colors in oil: white, black, vermilion, alizarin crimson, chrome yellow, yellow ocher, chrome green, permanent green, raw umber, burnt umber, Vandyke brown, Prussian blue

1 tube each of the following japan colors: light chrome yellow, yellow lake, brilliant green, azure blue, black, vermilion

1 pint flat white paint

1 pint asphalt varnish or paint

1 pint crude oil

6 ounces pumice

6 ounces rotten stone

1 roll each Nos. 1 and 2 steel wool

1 pint varnish remover

1 package or bottle each of the various shades of so-called "bronzing powders," such as lemon gold, deep gold, aluminum, copper

1 small piece of chamois

1 square yard tracing linen

2 square yards tracing paper

1 roll ½-inch Scotch tape

1 X-acto knife kit

1 pint carbon tetrachloride

1 pair embroidery scissors

1 soapstone pencil

While complete enough to set a beginner up in business, the list may have to be added to from time to time as we progress, become more confident, and begin to have our own ideas about things. This will be especially true of brushes and colors. As we move along in the work we shall become less and less dependent upon colors as they come from the tubes and shall wish to create our own shades. All of this will make for *original* work, pieces that are really ours in a more complete sense of the term than the result achieved by following printed directions. It is by color mixing that many artists achieve a great deal of their fame.

MIXING COLORS

There is, however, some rhyme and reason in color mixing. You will not want to mix indiscriminately any combinations of colors that come to mind. It is not the purpose of this book to deal extensively with the subject of color mixing, but a few words may help. The serious student who would like to enrich his knowledge on this subject is referred to any standard work on oil painting for the beginner.

There are certain rules of thumb about color that may be learned from a book, but each worker is advised to experiment with color mixing so that he may learn from actual experience. It should not take him long to discover that most colors mixed with white merely become diluted, that red and green become gray, and that the so-called "transparent colors" when mixed with the so-called "opaque colors" become far less transparent. He may have to relearn, too, such simple things as he learned in third or fourth grade: that yellow and blue become green, etc. Thus, if his manufactured green of standardized shade does not meet his specifications for leaves on a tray, he can mix his own, not just in one shade, but in as many different shades as he wishes.

Whereas some early stenciling that was overpainted in transparent colors and some early trays showed a certain subtlety in coloring, tinware painted commercially was usually quite crude. The order of the day, apparently, was to use as few colors as possible and to get them on in the simplest form. Little or no effort was made to shade such motifs as were used, the color being smeared on with solid blobs. A tomato was simply a large spot of red, and a leaf one or two blobs of green, just as it came from the can or palette.

There is no argument against decorating tinware in any manner that we wish or with degrees of refinement not achieved on the quaint old ware. However, if we choose to imitate old painting as accurately as possible, we must have no qualms about using solid color. We must remember, though, that this solid color cannot be produced with transparent oils or japan.

COLOR TRANSPARENCY

Finally a word about the basic nature of colors from the point of view of transparency: Some colors are utterly opaque when applied; they effectively screen off any hint of the color beneath them and do not change in shade when they are applied. Other colors are, in some measure at least, transparent when applied in moderate thicknesses. However, even transparent or semitransparent colors may approach opaqueness when applied in several coats. The paints considered most transparent are Prussian blue, mauve, verdigris, gamboge, and alizarin crimson. Partially transparent colors include yellow ocher, burnt umber, and burnt sienna.

All japan or oil colors may be mixed with the varnishes we shall be using. Indeed, this mixture is recommended in many cases—for example, to produce yellow paint for striping. Mixing any color with varnish will alter all the factors involved—color, transparency, fluidity, drying, etc. As a matter of fact, such mixing produces so many unexpected results that it might be well for each beginner to do a bit of experimental mixing before starting actual work. It is easy to mix a half teaspoonful of varnish with one of our colors and smear it on surfaces of various colors—black, deep brown, flat white, yellow. As we do this with each color we have at hand, the experience gained will be very worth while, especially if we make notes concerning the various effects. Experimenting in this way will also give us confidence.

I believe that each worker should strive for a certain independence in color where he is not attempting to make complete and authentic restorations or copies of the work on fancy chairs and other articles of furniture. All old-time stenciling did not slavishly follow a definite pattern where color was concerned. There was considerable variation. For instance, some gilders employed a transparent covering of oil paint to emphasize certain flower or fruit colors and subtle tones. Today some of these effects can be achieved with red, green, and blue powders which were not known in the early nineteenth century. While the beginner might well limit himself to plain bronze powder for his first few pieces, he may later wish to apply mixtures of Prussian blue and varnish to grapes, red and varnish to flowers, and green and varnish to leaves.

When colored oil paints are used over gold, bronze, or silver (aluminum) stencils, only small amounts need to be mixed in the following manner: Using 1 part of turpentine to 3 parts of varnish, add small amounts of color, whatever it may be, until the proper depth has been achieved. This will be determined by brushing a bit of the color over a bit of stencil to observe how transparent it is. If it is too deep and does not permit enough of the design to show through, it may be necessary to thin it with more varnish and turpentine. Only transparent colors are used in this work. Such colors are listed earlier in this chapter. In working with fruits and flowers, it will be found that the transparent colors alizarin, Prussian blue, and verdigris will meet most of our needs.

CHAPTER III

Copying and Cutting Stencils

WHILE ready-to-use stencils, copied from old designs, are available singly or in sets, most workers will wish to cut their own either from their own designs or from designs that have been traced from genuine old pieces of furniture. Once you master the slight skill needed to transfer these designs to suitable paper and to cut them, you will be guaranteed a never-ending supply of charming and original old designs. Chairs may always be borrowed for copying, or permission can be obtained from antique dealers to copy designs on chairs or other articles of furniture bearing suitable and worth-while work.

In many cases the article of furniture bearing the stencil desired for copying will be found in a grimy condition, having recently been pulled out of a hayloft or an attic. Covered with the accumulated dirt and grease of a century or more, it would seem impossible to uncover enough of the design for copying. However, if the design has not been badly damaged by scratches or scraping and has not been smeared with cheap varnish that has long since taken on a muddy appearance, there may be some chance of exposing enough of it for copying.

CLEANING OLD FURNITURE

The article of furniture, whatever it may be, is first given a good Saturday-night type of bath. For this bath, only clean water, Ivory flakes, and a trifle of boiled linseed oil are used. Special emphasis must be placed on the need for mild soap solutions in cleaning old stencil designs on furniture. Cheap yellow soaps intended for

18

laundry work and the detergent powders are not suitable. Where a design has worn thin, the use of powerful solvents or strong caustics may so badly damage what remains of the design as to render it completely or almost completely invisible through tracing paper or cloth. Mild Ivory flakes are by far best and safest.

While a gallon or more of water is warmed, enough soap flakes are added to produce, by agitation, a good sudsy solution. Then about a gill of boiled linseed oil is added, and the mixture is stirred.

Begin washing immediately, using clean rags and having the water–soap–linseed-oil solution as warm as can be comfortably borne by the hands.

For exceptionally heavy deposits of grime, a soft brush may accelerate removal. The use of a brush, however, should be limited to the cleaning of furniture that has an easily detectable film of old varnish over the stencil. If a part or all of the stencil has been left bare by the wearing away of its old varnish covering, use soft cloths instead of a brush. After a thorough washing, there should be considerable improvement in the visibility of the design. In most cases, you should be able to proceed with the job of tracing the design. If not, a further simple treatment with a 50-50 solution of boiled linseed oil and turpentine may produce results. This is applied with a clean rag, moistened with the solution just enough to leave a thin film. Any excess is removed gently with a second clean rag. If this does not bring out the design, there is nothing more that can be done.

In some cases where part of a design has become worn, it will not be visible when tracing cloth or paper is put in place. The visibility may be improved temporarily, for copying purposes, by going over the weak sections of the design with show-card paint of the right color—that is, a color that will show up best through the tracing medium. It should be a color that will stand out in contrast to the background. Show-card colors will not spoil the old design, for they can be easily removed with clean warm water and a clean rag.

MATERIAL FOR STENCILS

Several suitable materials are available for stencils and tracing. To avoid extra work in the form of needless retracing, the design should be traced directly on the translucent material from which the stencil is to be cut. Two materials suitable for stencils are commercially available. One is tracing linen, which is really fine Irish linen treated with starch to render it translucent enough for copying purposes. This linen is used by architects and mechanical draftsmen. It is not expensive; a few dollars' worth will keep you supplied for some time. It is durable, and once a design has been traced on it and cut, the resulting stencil may be used many times.

The other material is tracing paper, also used by architects and mechanical draftsmen. It costs only a few cents a yard and comes in 20-yard rolls under various trade names and in buff and white. I have found that a paper of medium grade or thickness is best. The heavy grade is too thick to be used on anything but the most prominent designs, and the very thin grade tears too easily. All such paper, because of its processing, is very brittle. Tracing paper is not so durable as linen, and your choice of materials should depend on whether you wish to use the stencil only once or a number of times. Linen is best, but paper stencils can be re-used if they are handled carefully. Torn paper stencils may be repaired easily with Scotch tape.

If you use tracing linen for copying, place the glossy side down (facing the design) and fasten the cloth to the chair, chest, or clock, as the case may be, with Scotch tape. In any case, whether you use cloth or paper, leave a margin of at least one inch, and preferably two, between the end of the design and the edge of the paper all the way around. This margin will help prevent smearing when powdered bronzes are used.

TRACING STENCILS

Tracing should be done with India drawing ink, of the kind used by draftsmen. The tracing is accomplished with a fine steel pen, and great care should be taken to draw the lines with a firm hand. Accuracy is essential. Here we should seek an arrangement that will permit as much relaxation as possible while the design is being traced. Awkward positions are tiring and quickly produce fatigue that makes accuracy impossible. For copying a design from a chair back, for instance, the chair may be laid flat on a bench or a table. The same holds true for clocks. In the case of a chest with stenciled drawers, remove the drawers and arrange them table-high so that they may be worked on conveniently.

If a design involves flourishes, curlicues, flamboyant scrolls, and fancy, symmetrical curves, as many of them do, we may find great assistance in a device used by draftsmen that is known as a "French curve." This is simply a piece of plastic, cut through with many different types of curves. It is placed on the paper or linen and is used to guide the pen. We will doubtless find on the French curve parts of many of those used in the design.

The corresponding parts of the French curve and the curve in the design are lined up with each other, giving the pen an accurate guide. These French curves come in different sizes and sets, and it is not too costly to purchase a whole set and have them near by when a design is being taken off.

After the design has been transferred to the paper or tracing

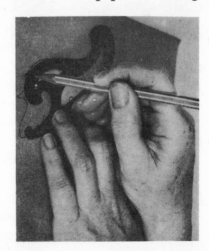

Fig. 8.   If the worker has a variety of French curves at hand, he will find them useful in tracing off and filling in the curves of old stencils that are being copied.

cloth, we are ready for the cutting, which must be done with extreme care. For this, some workers prefer a very sharp knife kept keenly honed on a very fine stone. A good-quality jackknife may serve the purpose. Some workers use the knives made for model-airplane builders. These come in kit form with a handle to which may be affixed a variety of steel blades. One such knife kit is sold under the trade name X-acto. Kept very sharp with a hone, such blades are very good for the work at hand. The kits are relatively inexpensive and may be purchased at any model-supply shop and at most hardware stores.

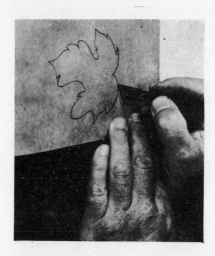

Fig. 9.   Using an X-acto knife in cutting a stencil unit from a good grade of tracing paper or tracing linen.

The careful worker, however, will use such equipment only with paper, the paper being placed on a semihard surface, such as a piece of Masonite, a form of composition wallboard available at any lumberyard. In cutting stencils, of course, we seek to make as clean an edge as possible. A ragged edge on the stencil will be faithfully reproduced on the finished work.

Knife cutting, while suitable for all grades of paper, has certain disadvantages when linen tracing cloth is used. Such cloth has linen fibers, and unless the knife is kept in an almost impossible condition of sharpness, it will leave slightly frayed edges. During cutting, the knife will tend to pull the fibers along with it as it moves, causing a slight fraying and thus destroying the sharpness of line that is needed in good stenciling.

For this reason, small embroidery or surgical scissors of the highest quality are recommended. As much of the cutting as possible should be done deep in the throat of the scissors.

Figure 10 illustrates the preferred method of using such scissors. Here the segment of a stencil for peaches is shown. The cross slits are cut with a knife. After these slits have been cut, it will be much easier to insert the scissors and cut into the traced lines. A clean-cut stencil should result. Here, too, a small honing stone should be kept at hand and used to touch up the scissor blades once in a while to keep them in top cutting form

Fig. 10. How embroidery scissors are started in cutting out a stencil. All of the cutting is done in the throat of the scissors to ensure clean edges in the tracing linen or tracing paper.

At times we come upon tiny circles in stencils where the scissors are too large to be effective. In such cases, we use the X-acto blade that comes to a very sharp point at the blade end. It may help prevent frayed edges if the linen is placed on a piece of glass while the tiny circles are being cut out.

And here "a word to the wise" may help. Most beginners make the mistake of being far too ambitious when they start tracing and cutting stencils. For the first few jobs, at least, we should not bite off even a little bit more than our experience will permit us to chew. We should select very simple stencils. Then we should reproduce them on test panels rather than on furniture that we expect to use. A few test panels can be fun, and they can also provide us with enough experience to go about the real work with greater confidence and skill. The trial panels can be done on small

Fig. 11. Original old-time stencils cut from letter paper. These are from the Cutting and Morrow Collection at the Metropolitan Museum of Art. (*Courtesy of the Metropolitan Museum of Art.*)

Fig. 12. An early nineteenth-century stencil from the Cutting and Morrow Collection at the Metropolitan Museum of Art. (*Courtesy of the Metropolitan Museum of Art.*)

Fig. 13. A variety of old stencils with floral motifs. Sometimes these were multiunit stencils, and sometimes all the design components were included in a single sheet of paper. These selections were made from the Cutting and Morrow Collection at the Metropolitan Museum of Art. (*Courtesy of the Metropolitan Museum of Art.*)

pieces of Masonite painted a dull black. Here the preparatory procedures are the same as those which will be described in connection with the preparation for work on furniture.

Some old stencils are very elaborate and very complicated, requiring a number of combinations of stencils (involving seven

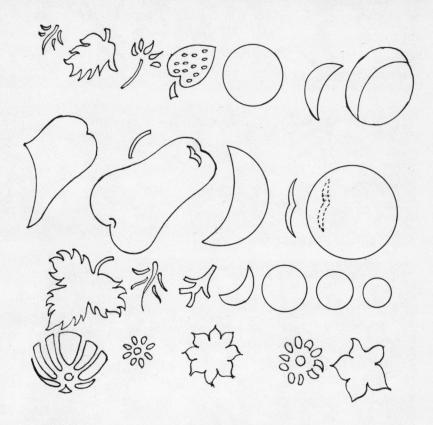

Fig. 14. Various other motifs and components of multiunit stencils.

or eight pieces). These are difficult to trace and cut without experience. This is another argument for the slower but surer approach by way of the test panels. And then if such panels reveal our skill, they are often attractive enough to hang in studio or bedroom for decoration.

Both tracing paper and tracing linen are susceptible to moisture, even to excessive atmospheric dampness on a very humid day. Once they become badly exposed, they will wrinkle and warp and never return to their original condition. If there is anything that a good stencil artist insists upon, it is a stencil that will lie perfectly flat and snug on the surface that is to be decorated. Hence, when not in use, all stencils should be stored flat in a closed box and kept in a dry place. So kept, they will be serviceable for many years and may be used over and over again.

CHAPTER IV

Stencil Motifs

FOR CERTAIN authentic pieces of old furniture you will want to use old designs copied from other pieces. Yet I have never felt that it is necessary always to follow old patterns. Striking out boldly on your own and adapting the old symbols and motifs to your own design can bring a great deal of creative satisfaction. The development of new and original designs is not too difficult, especially if you study the stencil motifs that were used in the early nineteenth century.

I am not suggesting that old forms be avoided, but I am proposing that you try variations or adaptations of old designs. Thus, instead of merely copying work that has already been done, you will be exercising your own skill, ingenuity, and artistic talent.

Unfortunately, not all of the motifs used have been catalogued. Some, such as the locomotive and train of cars I once saw on an old tray, were used only rarely. The locomotive was of the type used in the late 1830s and early 1840s. I have also seen a tray with a canalboat on its stencil form. It is natural that the artist-craftsman who designed stencils a hundred years ago should have been inspired by two of the great wonders of his day. These unusual designs are interesting and attractive and lend themselves easily to stencilmaking. From old pictures of early railroad trains and packet boats you can evolve a stencil for use on tray bottoms.

NATURALISTIC MOTIFS

Many were the naturalistic motifs employed in stenciling, most of them from the plant world. The leaf in several forms appeared consistently and even monotonously. The carved acanthus leaf was widely used on mahogany furniture of the late American Empire period, but the stenciled leaf more often represented other vegetation. Sometimes it was a leaf form born out of the imagination of the stencilmakers. Sometimes leaves appeared with stems, sometimes without; rarely did they appear in full. As a matter of fact, it is rare to find any naturalistic motif appearing in full, save for an occasional flower or a piece of fruit.

Like leaves, some flowers were recognizable, others bore little or no relation to anything in the floral kingdom. Here and there one is able to recognize a daisy or a rose and, in rarer cases, a tulip or a morning-glory.

All forms of fruit that were used are more easily identified. The most prominent and widely employed were the peach, the grape, and the melon. The apple is rarely seen; and although the pineapple motif, symbol of hospitality, was widely used in carved mahogany furniture of the Empire era, it is not often found in stencils. The reason is not too difficult to discover. It would have taken a rare genius to have devised a simple stencil for the reproduction of the pineapple. The leafage of the top would have been easy enough, but the pin-eyed surface of the fruit would have offered a difficult problem. Plums and cherries were widely used in various sizes and segments.

Finished designs were sometimes combinations of fruit and flowers, all flowers and leaves, or all fruit and leaves. This is not to say that all designs followed this rule, but most of the conventional ones did. Oftentimes a cornucopia with fruit issuing from it was used.

Here and there one finds the shell motif, but it is rare and appears more often on trays than on the splats of chairs or on other furniture. Of course, the shell was a little more difficult to handle in a stencil than were some of the other naturalistic motifs employed. More skill was required to make a shell than to make a strawberry or a spiral form; hence the scarcity. Those who used the shell were obviously influenced by the rococo designs of late eighteenth-century France.

Fig. 15. Floral motifs skillfully employed with leaves and sprays. These are single-piece stencils with no overlapping components. (*Courtesy of the Metropolitan Museum of Art.*)

Fig. 16. Excellent use of the peach, apple, plum, leaf, cornucopia, and compote motifs in the decoration of an 1825 shelf-clock cornice.

Fig. 17. The shell motif employed on a stencil of the early 1820s. This motif was little used on furniture but widely used on trays. (*Courtesy of the Metropolitan Museum of Art.*)

ANIMAL MOTIFS

If animal motifs were used by the stencilmakers, I have never seen them. Apparently animals were not reproduced either because the stencil did not lend itself well to such creatures or because the artists and craftsmen of the day were not skillful enough to adapt the stencil to these representations. Often, of course, one finds the American eagle on trays, but rarely upon chair splats, although the Federal nationalistic feeling was still intense during the early years of the stencil.

It has been my casual observation that buildings and scenes began to be used on wide chair slats, especially on top slats of Boston rockers, during the 1840s and later. These take the forms of old castles, churches, street scenes, etc., often with such addi-

Fig. 18. Building motifs used to decorate the top rail of a Boston rocker made in the late 1830s. (*Courtesy of Miss Florence E. Wright.*)

Fig. 19. The Aeolian or harp motif. While not widely employed, it did show up on fancy chairs intended for use in music rooms. (*Courtesy of the Metropolitan Museum of Art.*)

tional details as people and trees. Usually the trees and other foliage were painted in with a brush. Picturesque bridges over streams were also employed, and they were often given their finishing touches with brushes without benefit of stencils.

Of course the urn and the compote were widely used in stenciling, but not as motifs. The compote usually held fruit, whereas the urn in various forms was employed solely as a holder for flowers.

BORDERS

Borders took any number of forms from the simple stripe (not so simple to execute!) to the projected points of leaves. Usually borders were composed of simple geometric forms, such as combinations of short lines (dashes), triangles, circles, etc. Some were so far removed from conventional forms that it is difficult to name them or to assign a category to them.

Stenciled representations of fountains were used, especially on trays. Baskets, too, were occasionally employed.

While discussing motifs, it might be well to mention briefly the layout and arrangement of designs and the appropriateness of certain designs for certain pieces of furniture.

SIZE OF STENCILS

First of all, a design should be produced with an eye to the space into which it must fit, in relation not only to shape but also to size. We must try to avoid an overcrowded effect. Many old designs failed in this respect, especially on chair slats and splats, thus detracting from their artistic appeal. For example, we should not carry a design to the edge of the space allotted to it. Certain parts of a design may be allowed near the edge, but not all of it. The best work in the old days had a considerable border of plain color or black between it and the edge of the space upon which it was painted or stenciled.

There is an artistic effect to be achieved also in creating a design to fit the type or style of furniture on which it is to be used. For instance, a design that might be used on the headboard of an 1825 four-poster bed probably would not be suitable for one of the more delicate fancy chairs of the same period; it would be too heavy. However, the same motifs might be used on a chair, but in a smaller size and with much less mass.

We should also avoid overcomplicated designs—a mistake sometimes made by the stencilers of old. Intricate designs made up of different and often unrelated motifs are far less pleasing than simpler forms.

In many cases design should be based upon geography. For example, we should not place a typical Hitchcock or New England type of stencil on a Pennsylvania-type plank-seat chair, nor should we use a Pennsylvania Fraktur-inspired decoration on a Connecti-cut-type dower chest. The Pennsylvania Dutch chair was painted rather than stenciled and, Dutch-like, the tulip motif was often employed.

Background is also an important factor. Chairs were painted green, yellow, black, and deep brown. Thus, the colors used in the designs must be controlled in some measure by background colors to produce pleasing contrasts that will show off the designs to best advantage.

Finally, in addition to producing the most suitable artistic effects, we shall also seek to give our work the stamp of authenticity in color, design, and skillful workmanship.

CHAPTER V

Stripping and Restoring
Old Furniture

IF YOU INTEND to apply stencils to antiques, you will want to know how to remove finishes and how to rehabilitate old pieces of furniture. Most old Hitchcock-type chairs, for instance, reach the antique market after having lost their last shred of design, or with so little of it left that there is no alternative to getting down to the clean, bare wood where we can start fresh with a virgin surface.

But first a word about rehabilitation: Before we decide to repair a wobbly, seatless old chair—or, indeed, before we decide to discard it as beyond repair—let us make sure that it is in need of such attention. These old relics sometimes fool us. I have often come upon chairs which look as if the rungs or stretchers could easily be yanked out of their sockets and as if the joints were desperately in need of regluing. Closer examination will often reveal that the joint cannot be so easily separated and that a new rush seat will eliminate the wobbly condition almost entirely.

The old chairmakers had a simple technique for establishing firm, lasting joints between the stretchers or rungs and the legs. Partially green, or unseasoned, wood was used for the legs, while the stretchers were turned from carefully seasoned wood. Therefore, after a tight joint was made, the unseasoned legs continued to shrink and after a few years they so firmly gripped the ends of the rungs that the joints have lasted to this very day. No glue was employed.

Although these joints may appear weak in a seatless chair, it is best to leave them alone, with the assurance that once a good tight seat is placed on the chair, most if not all of the wobble will disappear. Those of us without experience will be amazed at the way in which a chair is strengthened by the installation of a new seat of cane, rush, or splat. More instructions concerning repair will be given later in this chapter. The first job is to remove the paint and varnish.

REMOVING PAINT

The thrifty person who would remove paint in the cheapest way with a piece of broken glass and a solution of hot lye is warned against such a procedure on several counts. First, there is the danger of cutting one's hands seriously and of having the sharp edge of the glass cut deeply into the wood. However, it is in the hot lye that the real danger lies, both to the human flesh and to the wood. True, such a highly corrosive solution will quickly cut into old paint and varnish, but it will cut just as quickly and just as deeply into skin, producing ugly burns that are long in healing. There is also the risk that a drop of lye may be splashed into the eye with fatal results to sight. Aside from these dangers, lye attacks the wood fibers, making them soft and spongy; and unless all the lye solution is completely eliminated, it may later come through the finish and spoil a good job which has taken hours of patient work.

It is best and safest by far to purchase a quart or two of one of the modern paint and varnish removers. These may be in liquid or paste form. Choice is optional with the worker; both are good. Perhaps the paste is a little safer to use, because you are not so likely to splash it on clothing or into your eyes. Such an accident can have very serious consequences unless this powerful solvent is washed out immediately. When using paint remover, I always wear a pair of cheap goggles. In addition to these precautions, follow the directions on the can or bottle and work in a well-ventilated room because of the toxic nature of the vapor from such solvents and because of the dangerous fire risks involved when the atmosphere becomes saturated with their vapor. Also avoid, as far as possible, actual contact with these solvents, which are so powerful that they instantly dissolve out the fatty matter in the skin and penetrate the pores to some extent, thereafter being picked up by the blood stream.

When applying paint and varnish remover to furniture, it is best to work on flat, horizontal surfaces. For instance, when varnish is being removed from the back of a chair, the chair back should be laid flat on a bench. This permits the solvent to attack the varnish or paint in greater volume; if the surface is vertical, the solvent runs off almost as fast as it is applied.

When removing varnish or paint on carved legs, place the leg in a tin can or a dish and keep washing the carved part with the solution. A stiff toothbrush will help remove the varnish or paint from the crevices of the carving.

When varnish is being removed from the fronts of bureau drawers or other such places adjacent to wood that has no covering (the sides of drawers), take care that the varnish- or paint-saturated fluid does not run off onto the virgin wood, where it will immediately penetrate and stain.

On perfectly flat surfaces, use a broad putty knife to scrape off paint or varnish after it has been thoroughly loosened by the solvent. Use an ordinary jackknife for scraping chair stretchers and rungs.

SCRAPING PAINT

Dry removal of paint or varnish is possible with a steel scraper. It is much more difficult than the use of solvents, however, and is likely to damage the surface of the wood. Scrapers must be very sharp, and when removing old, hard paint from, say, a chest of drawers we might have to resharpen the blade many times. And with a sharp blade there is always the danger of producing a deep gouge that will be difficult to repair.

REMOVING WAX

One more precaution may be illustrated by citing the experience of a neighbor of mine: Inheriting an old family chest of drawers, the neighbor came to me for information about the best method of paint removal. A few days later he returned with the complaint that, although three days had passed since he had varnished his prize, the varnish was still almost as wet as it was when he put it on and the chest had gathered a disgusting amount of dust. He was pretty well discouraged.

I asked him if he had remembered to wash off the chest with a 50-50 solution of turpentine and untreated gasoline after he had removed the varnish. Come to think of it, he had not. That was the source of his trouble.

All paint and varnish removers contain large amounts of wax or paraffin. These waxes dissolve out and deposit themselves on the wood surfaces after the paint or varnish has been taken off. The waxes thereby prevent the solvents from penetrating the pores of the wood to damage the wood fibers by dissolving out their natural oils. To eliminate these waxes, you must first sandpaper with fine paper and then wipe carefully with a clean rag saturated with the gasoline-turps mixture. Otherwise the wax will plug the pores and prevent penetration of the varnish; it will also associate itself with the oil in the varnish and prevent evaporation. When confronted with such a problem, the only solution is a second complete removal, remembering this time to take the precautions noted.

REPAIRING CHAIR JOINTS

If you find that a chair really needs repairing, now is the time to do it. You will remember the advice given earlier never to yank out a rung-leg joint unless it seems about ready to separate itself. A bit of airplane cement or ordinary glue will not reestablish this joint. If we are to smear the joint with anything, it should be a good grade of prepared glue. Even smearing it on, pushing the rung end back into the socket, and letting the joint stand until the

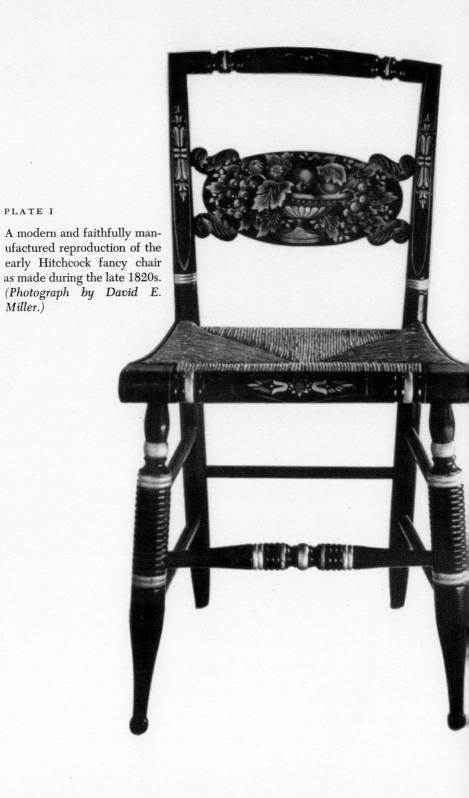

PLATE I

A modern and faithfully manufactured reproduction of the
early Hitchcock fancy chair
as made during the late 1820s.
(Photograph by David E.
Miller.)

glue dries will not do. The chair must be wired with baling wire so as to bring great pressure on the joint or joints so treated. This is done with tourniquets. Incidentally, you will waste your time if you use rope instead of baling wire. When rope is placed under such a stress as will be needed here, it will stretch just enough to become useless.

Glue smeared over an old glued joint will not give you the strength you need. To be effective, glue must penetrate the pores of the wood in both joined surfaces. That means scrupulously clean wood; nothing short of this will do. Therefore we have to scrape away all old glue before fresh glue is put in place. This may be done with a small sharp knife. Glue will be found in such joints only if the chair has been repaired before, inasmuch as the old chairmakers never used glue.

Unless the joint is tight, we shall be wasting our time in applying an adhesive. Some instructions on repairs of this sort recommend using a bit of tape around the end of a chair rung before it is glued. This, too, is a procedure that can only lead to eventual disappointment. Such a joint may hold for a time, but in the long run it will loosen. If a joint is not tight enough to necessitate driving the rung in with a mallet after the glue is applied, then other means of repair should be called upon.

Figure 20 illustrates an approved method of repair of too loose a joint. Here, however, we must achieve complete accuracy. There must be a certain relationship between the V cut in the rung end and the small wedge inserted in it. The wedge must be the same length as the depth of the V and of sufficient thickness in its end portion to expand the end of the rung slightly when it is driven home with a mallet into the socket of the chair leg. It is advisable to smear the wedge and the V with glue before the driving is done. Don't be alarmed when most of the glue oozes out of the joint when the rung is driven into the leg hole or socket; this is a sign of a good joint. A large amount of glue left in a joint indicates that it is not tight enough.

If you have at your disposal some of the large steel clamps used by cabinetmakers in making glued butt joints, they may be used in gluing chairs. Indeed, they are preferable to baling wire. In either case, the points of contact are wrapped with old rags so that the pressure created by the wires or the jaws of the clamps will not cause them to bite into the wood and leave a mark.

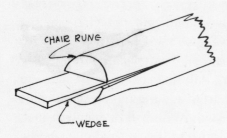 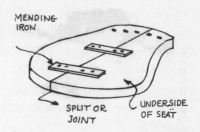

Fig. 20. Details of an expanded joint repair for a chair rung. The joint should be smeared with a good grade of glue before it is driven in place with a mallet.

Fig. 21. Splits in the seats of all-wooden chairs are repaired with glue and clamps. Mending irons placed as illustrated should preserve the joint for many years.

REPAIRING CHAIR SEATS

Clamps are necessary when repairing the seats of Pennsylvania Dutch–type stenciled or painted chairs. Although the plank seats were usually cut from a single board, they will be found to have developed splits over the years. The surfaces should be covered with glue, and the clamps applied. As added insurance, we apply a mending iron (6-inch type) to the bottom of such chairs (see Fig. 21). These irons are available in hardware stores.

What about the old chair relic with one half of its stencils in good shape and the other half all but obliterated? Is it possible to restore the bad half? Perhaps, with several years of experience and more than ordinary skill, we might try such restoration; otherwise the odds are hopelessly against success.

However, if more than half of the design can still be seen, we should never pass up an opportunity at least to trace the design on tracing paper and add it to our collection. Part of the fun of stenciling is to build up a collection of old stencil designs.

CHAPTER VI

Undercoatings and Backgrounds

AGAIN, as in Chapter V, "Stripping and Restoring Old Furniture," we shall refer mostly to chairs in describing techniques, although much of the data may be used in the preparation of suitable backgrounds for the stenciling of other furniture, such as beds, chests, and clocks. These articles of furniture invariably had dead black backgrounds for their stencils, but this dull black was rarely, if ever, used on early stenciled chairs. Chairs were for the most part gayer, with yellow, pearl-gray, or green backgrounds. By far the widest range of background colors was employed on fancy chairs. A chest with stencil decorations simply had black drawer fronts over which the stencils were placed. Clocks had stencil-decorated pilasters and cornices. Mirrors had only decorated pilasters, and it was the foot- and headboards of beds that carried the designs.

An expert and satisfactory job of painting and stenciling requires a suitable surface upon which to place our paint and varnish. Hence, after the old finish has been removed according to the directions in Chapter V, we make minor repairs in the wood surfaces and then sandpaper thoroughly.

FILLING CRACKS

Should it be necessary to fill any deep cracks or gouges, we may employ plastic wood for the purpose so long as paint will be used for covering. In cases where only transparent varnish is to be used, plastic wood is not recommended for repairs for the simple reason that it provides a nonabsorbent surface and will therefore produce a color quite different from that of the surrounding surface. It is possible, however, to color plastic wood or other types of crack

41

filler to match the wood, but it is difficult to obtain a perfect match.

In a few cases when refinishing chairs that were produced in the 1850s and 1860s (which were jet-black originally), we shall find a deep penetration of color. If we are going to finish these chairs in dark colors, this residue of the old black need not concern us, but for other finishes it is advisable to use a scraper before sanding in order to remove all traces of the original paint.

USING SANDPAPER

After all blemishes have been removed or repaired, we may proceed to the sandpapering, remembering that the quality of any refinished article can be no better than the quality of the wood surface, so far as smoothness is concerned. For those who have never sandpapered before, it may be said that we must always follow the grain of the wood. With a chair in a standing position, this means that we must move back and forth (horizontally) on slats and up and down (vertically) on splats. For rungs and stretchers, cut the sandpaper into strips about 1½ inches wide, wrap them around the rungs or stretchers, and work back and forth. Any violation of this rule about following the grain will only produce ugly scratches in the wood, which are difficult to remove.

We start with a relatively coarse paper, like No. 1, and wind up with No. 00. This may be followed with an application of steel wool until the surface is as smooth as glass. Finally we wipe the wood with a slightly dampened cloth to remove all the wood dust that may be clinging to the surface.

After complete and thorough sanding, some workers apply a thin coat of shellac (50 per cent shellac and 50 per cent denatured alcohol) before applying the first coat of background paint. If this application is made (I take a neutral position on this), it will be necessary to go over the shellacked surface with steel wool.

PROPER BRUSHES

As I mentioned in Chapter II, good finishes cannot be produced with cheap brushes. We should purchase the best quality brush available and take good care of it. A brush 1 or 1½ inches wide will be satisfactory for small articles of furniture such as chairs. These brushes usually come with the bristles wrapped in oiled paper. If they are not so wrapped, they should be washed in clean turpentine before being used, for dust is the ever-present villain for the refinisher.

It is also necessary to take good care of our brushes between coats. After use, they should be washed out, superficially at least, and then placed in a jar of clean turpentine, as illustrated in Fig. 22. Upon removal for re-use, they should be swished violently to remove the excess turpentine and then wiped with a clean, lint-less rag.

Above all, the careful worker will not permit a brush to stand with its bristles down in an open can of paint or varnish until he is ready for his second coat. The open can will accumulate dust, and the contents will tend to oxidize, with the consequent formation of a thin film of paint or varnish on the surface.

After a job is completed, it is best to clean the brush well with a series of pure turpentine baths before putting it away. After the last turpentine bath, as much as possible of the residual color is wiped out with a clean rag. The brush is given a final bath in a warm, sudsy soap solution, after which it is wiped again with a clean, lintless rag. The brush is then set to dry in a dustless compartment and is finally wrapped in waxed paper. This procedure will preserve a brush for an indefinite period. Otherwise, color that remains will plague us in future use, and a hard accumulation of paint or varnish will be deposited in the heel of the brush.

What about the use of modern solvent brush cleaners? So far as I am concerned, there appears to be no special advantage in their use. They are efficient, to be sure, in the removal of paint and varnish. But they are relatively expensive, and their fumes are toxic and also dangerous as a possible fire hazard. Some experts

Fig. 22. Brushes may be preserved for long use by keeping them in a covered jar filled with kerosene or turpentine to a point above the bristles.

feel that brush cleaners may damage good brushes by dissolving too much natural oil out of the bristles.

USING MODERN LACQUERS

Now, before beginning to paint, let me answer another question that may come up: Can modern lacquers be used in refinishing old furniture? Is it advisable to employ them? The answer is in the affirmative so far as a beautiful and lasting finish is concerned. But if we insist on finishes that resemble old finishes, the answer is no. The answer is also negative with regard to ease of application, for lacquer sets up with uncompromising speed. There is no possibility of going back to touch up a weep or a run or a rough spot after a few moments have elapsed. Such touching up would only roll up the lacquer and create a major problem quite beyond the solution of the amateur refinisher.

If we do not care to follow old finishing routines so diligently, and if we are pleased with the lacquer finish after taking into consideration the difficulties mentioned above, then there can be no objection to its use. As a matter of fact, because of its terrific speed in drying dust-free in a few moments' time, there is no dust problem with lacquer. However, it does require a certain technique with a brush, inasmuch as it must be flowed on rather than brushed on, and flowing it greatly emphasizes the weeping problem and the problem of the formation of tears on the bottoms of chair rungs.

If lacquer is to be used, it is best to spray it on, applying several coats in very fine sprays. The home vacuum-cleaner spray attachment may be used for this purpose. Lacquer dries so rapidly that several coats may be put on within the space of a few hours.

Of course, the use of lacquer or, indeed, of any modern enamel would be frowned upon by those who will not deviate from the methods and materials used a hundred years ago. The controlling factor, of course, should be what the worker wants and is satisfied with. If he considers the effect of lacquer or enamel satisfactory, then lacquer or enamel it should be.

If you look closely at the really old fancy chairs that appear to be black, you will notice that they are not solid black but rather a combination of black and red, with the red (Venetian or Chinese in shade) showing through in streaks in the manner of the artificially grained woodwork in 1890 homes where a rubber comb was used to streak fresh brown paint or varnish to make the undercoating show through. If anything, the finish looks more like a surface artificially created to resemble rosewood. Some of this old graining with black and red finish on chairs was done very carefully, and some, more carelessly executed, was rather crude.

RED UNDERCOATING

But more about graining later. What we are interested in at the moment is the application of the first red undercoating if the grained finish is what we are aiming for. Some workers mix their own red undercoating; some purchase red paint and apply it with or without color adjustments made by adding oil-ground pigments. What you want to avoid for these red background coverings is glossy or semiglossy enamels of any kind. There is nothing wrong with house paint of the right color so long as it is thinned down considerably with turpentine and applied in two coats. If it is thinned enough to be applied with the home vacuum-cleaner spraying equipment, so much the better. Three coats applied in this way will do no harm, although two should be sufficient.

So far as I am aware, no paint manufacturer produces the particular shade of barn red, Chinese red, or Venetian red that was used on old chairs. It is a pretty safe bet, then, that each worker will have to create his own shade from home-mixed materials. To achieve such a color, in approximation at least, we mix some japan vermilion, japan dark red, and a bit of burnt umber in oil. Concentrated japan colors come in small tubes similar to the tubes in which artists' oil colors come, and also in cans. Inasmuch as we shall use relatively small amounts of these colors, and because the surface of japan colors oxidizes very rapidly, we shall choose the collapsible tube rather than the can. The same holds for the colors mixed in oil which, by the way, may also be mixed with japan colors as suggested above.

The mixture of japan vermilion, japan red, and burnt umber in oil to produce Chinese or barn red should be effected in a solution of varnish thinned considerably with turpentine. While we are mixing it, we should be sure that we have prepared enough for two coats. A bit of treatment with fine steel wool or 00 sandpaper will help build up a smooth undersurface. The smoother each succeeding coat is, the finer the last surface will be. Twenty-four hours of drying should be allowed for each coat of undercovering, whether it is red, black, or flat white, the last of which is used when fancy chairs are to be finished in pearl gray, yellow, or light green.

Inasmuch as several coats of varnish will be placed over the coat of black that is painted over the red undercoating, the black may be either dull or semiglossy. It must be "grained" immediately after it is applied and while it is still very wet. If this is not done before the black paint has had a chance to set up slightly, we shall have occasion to regret a sad-looking and unsatisfactory job.

Before any graining is done, it would be well to examine an old chair done in this fashion to see how much red shows through the black and to note the degree of the undulating, or wavy, effect because the old graining was never in perfectly straight lines.

The graining may be achieved with any one of several suitable materials: crumpled paper, cheesecloth or mosquito netting, burlap, etc. Even a dry paintbrush, if lightly applied, may be used. The aim is to remove some of the black so that thin streaks or lines of the red undercoating will show through. After the correct effect has been achieved, it is left to dry.

Careful examination of old chairs finished in this manner fails to show any sign of graining on the slats or splats. Although the red undercoating may have been used, these parts of chairs were not grained. No doubt this was because this effect might have detracted from the stencils which were applied to slats and splats. It should be an invariable rule with amateur refinishers and stencilers of old chairs that slats (horizontal members) or splats (vertical members) of chair backs should never be grained but should be painted a solid color.

When the chair is dry, you are ready to apply the stencil.

LIGHT BACKGROUNDS

Although by far the larger percentage of the later fancy chairs (from 1820 on) were prepared for stenciling in the manner just described, a considerable number were painted with lighter-colored backgrounds. Some of these were prepared for hand-painted designs, some for stencils. Among the colors employed were bone ivory, light green, pearl gray, and yellow. If you wish to apply these lighter finishes, the procedure is the same as that followed in applying the basic coats of red—two coats, plus treatment with steel wool or fine sandpaper in between coats. No black paint or graining is used.

Of course, the easiest way would be to go to the nearest paint shop and purchase a can of enamel which suits your taste so far as color is concerned. It will be better, however, to take a bit of time to concoct your own mixture, which may be more in conformity with the exact shades you have in mind, and it can be prepared from ingredients that are usually available even in small-town paint stores.

You will need the following materials: turpentine, white lead, japan and oil colors, and either 24-hour or 4-hour Super-Valspar varnish.

You may need to experiment considerably with small amounts before you achieve the color you want among the yellows, grays, or greens. At any rate, start your mixing with clear varnish to which a fairly large quantity of flat white is added. To this mixture add the colors, whatever they may be. For instance, the gray you wish may be produced by adding black and blue; or the yellow by adding yellow ocher and a bit of burnt umber. Compared to the total volume of the completed mixture, only very small amounts of coloring, either in oil or japan, will be needed. The final consistency should be about the same as that of ordinary commercial enamel. Turpentine may be added as a reducing agent.

Stenciling procedures are the same as for darker backgrounds, although the choice of metallic-powder colors may be influenced by the lighter backgrounds in order to achieve a satisfactory contrast.

CHAPTER VII

Applying Stencils

ANYONE CAN slap paint on a piece of furniture, but there are some who would hesitate to apply a stencil design to a chair or a tin tray. Perhaps you can't achieve, the first time you try, the results of the craftsmen of the early nineteenth century; they were highly skilled workmen, and their skill, modest as it was, cannot be mastered overnight by reading this or any other book. But with practice you can gain the experience that will permit you to tackle your first chair with the kind of confidence that makes for good results.

I cannot too strongly recommend the painting of a number of test panels to achieve this experience. They are prepared in a less exacting manner than chairs or other pieces of furniture, and the small amount of time and effort required will be amply repaid in more perfect finished work.

Most satisfactory for test panels are small pieces of ⅛-inch Masonite wallboard available at any lumberyard. Oftentimes small scrap strips may be purchased for a few cents. For satisfactory practice we ought to prepare at least ten panels before we try a single chair. Each panel is given a coat of shellac. Then it is given a coat of flat black and is put away to dry, after which it is varnished.

VARNISH FOR STENCILING

Gold or bronze stencils are not painted with a brush. The metallic powders that are used are pressed into a second coat of varnish while the varnish is in the tacky stage of drying. A knowledge of exactly the right time for applying the stencil can be gained only by experience—another reason for experimenting and practicing on test panels. One of the problems is that we run into two variable factors which control the drying rate of varnish. If the humidity is high (80 to 90 per cent) and the temperature relatively low (50 to 60 degrees), drying to the point of tackiness will be slow. On the other hand, if the temperature is above 70 degrees and the humidity below 60 per cent, conditions will be ideal for fast drying. You may, therefore, want to wait for these ideal atmospheric conditions before beginning your work. If you plan to do a lot of stenciling, it will pay to have in your finishing room an instrument that registers the percentage of humidity in the atmosphere.

The varnish should be of the conventional type—*not one of the modern mixtures involving a number of synthetic materials.* It is pretty safe to stick to Valentine products, either the regular or the Super. Although there is a wide variation in drying periods between the two, this is not important so long as you can determine the degree of tackiness required for stenciling. This should be a point at which the pad of a finger may be pressed down upon the varnish with moderate pressure and pulled away (1) without much tendency to stick and (2) without leaving fingerprints on the surface of the varnish. Depending upon the nature of the varnish and upon the atmospheric conditions, from one to several hours may pass before this ideal condition is reached.

Naturally, this ideal stage will not last all day; if the day is good for quick drying, the tackiness may pass completely before we have finished our work. What, then, should we do? There is only one answer to that: We must revarnish and again wait for the tacky stage. No harm will be done, and while we are about it we can varnish over the part of the stencil that we have completed.

HOW TO HANDLE VARNISH

Now a word about varnish for those who have had no experience with it: Although paints and enamels have to be stirred or shaken to mix the precipitated color pigment in the bottom of the can, this procedure is not necessary with varnish; in fact, varnish should never be shaken or stirred. Such action only mixes air with it, and the air will appear on the varnished surface in the form of bubbles. And bubbles can be mean! For the same reason we should not pour varnish so that it gurgles from the small spout of a gallon can.

Varnish can be made a bit more liquid and thus easier to flow upon a surface if it is heated slightly in a double boiler. Direct heating will spoil the varnish, and in no case should varnish reach a temperature higher than 120 degrees Fahrenheit.

In working on a chair—or any other surface—we do not take a full brush of varnish. Instead, the brush—which should not be more than 1 or 1½ inches in width—is dipped into the varnish only halfway down the bristles, and the excess varnish is then wiped off on the edge of the can. Excessive application only increases the drying time, which in turn increases the dust problem and the danger of tears on the bottoms of the rungs and weeps on the slats or splats.

Remember, too, that an old, dirty brush will only cause disappointment in your work. It is not only that such a brush may carry a bit of color from previous use, but also that it will have in its bristles bits of hard paint or dust because it has not been properly cared for. Your varnish brush should be used for varnish exclusively. After each job it should be rinsed in clean turpentine, washed in a warm, sudsy solution of water and Ivory flakes, and wrapped in waxed paper.

Dust, of course, is not limited to dirty brushes. It may also come from dusty clothes, cellar ceilings that constantly rain dust particles as a result of the walking on floors above, dusty surroundings, open windows, etc. I suggest that you wipe everything with a damp cloth before you start to varnish and that you wear freshly laundered clothes. Dust pimples on a varnished surface cannot be eliminated with steel wool or sandpaper after the varnish is dry. Nor will several coats of varnish applied over stencils cover up dust marks. The dust must be kept off in the first place; there is no other solution. Remember that dust will rob even the most perfect piece of stenciling of its deserved beauty.

APPLYING BRONZE POWDER

We are now ready to apply stencils to our test panels. You will find that if the varnish is tacky enough to hold the metallic powders, it will also be tacky enough to hold the stencil itself and to prevent its shifting if you press the stencil down gently when you put it in place.

The finely divided metallic powders used in bronzing, gilding, and silvering are made up of particles so small that they may become air-borne in slight drafts, and thus they may be carried to surfaces where they do not belong. Work carefully to prevent these particles from reaching sticky varnished surfaces outside the area of the stencil.

Another way in which these powders cause trouble is by seeping underneath the cut edges of stencils, where they blur sharp outlines and may so smudge a design as to spoil it. Much, if not all, of this trouble can be avoided if you carefully run the pad of a finger over the edges of the stencil after it has been placed on the tacky varnish. This will seal the edges against the intrusion of powder when the powder is being applied. With a delicate stencil, the pad of the finger should simply be pressed down progressively to produce a temporary but tight bond between the stencil and the tacky varnished surface.

Smudging and a generally messy result may also mar your work if the surplus metallic powder is not carefully wiped away from the stencil with a turpentine-moistened rag just before the stencil is removed. If this is not done, a whole shower of such particles may descend upon the unstenciled varnished surface which could still be tacky enough to catch them and hold them. Such a catastrophe can spoil a piece of work to such an extent that the careful worker would hesitate to show it as a sample of his skill.

If you are working with a large and complicated stencil and feel that you will not be able to complete your work in about one-half hour's time or before the varnish has lost its critical degree of tackiness, then you should work in restricted areas and complete them before moving along to new areas. This method will help if you have to revarnish to reestablish another tacky surface.

If at all possible, surfaces to which stencils are being applied should be in a horizontal position. This will prevent overdoses of the metallic powder from drifting downward and catching underneath any slight opening that may exist between the stencil and the surfaces to which it is affixed.

HANDLING BRONZE POWDERS

Now a few words about these metallic powders before we begin using them on our test panels: First, we should not make the mistake of trying to economize by picking up the cheapest powders available. Instead, we should ask our paint dealer for the very best, and if he does not have them in stock, we should ask him to order them for us. Reasonable amounts (½- or 1-ounce packages) are not so expensive as to preclude the possibility of our putting in a complete supply of all colors at the time we make our original purchase. Although different manufacturers give different names to their colors, we shall want to have on hand a supply of gold-leaf powder, brushed brass, silver or "aluminum bronze," as it is called, fire bronze or red, green, and blue. The last two colors will probably not be used frequently, but so long as we are ordering, we may just as well have a complete kit.

It is convenient to transfer these powders from their original containers, which may be bottles or small envelopes, to small cardboard or tin pill or salve boxes. Round, shallow tin boxes about 3 inches in diameter make ideal containers. Such boxes are usually available at drugstores, where they are used for putting up salves and ointments.

As discussed earlier, when the varnish has reached the tacky stage, you are ready to make your first attempt at applying a stencil to a test panel. Even though it is a test panel, you will want to follow precisely all the rules of the game. The first requirement is that the stencil be mounted exactly in the center of the panel. After all, if you were applying a stencil to a chair slat and found, after the work had been completed, that one end was ½ inch higher than the other and that the slant was easily noticeable, you would not be very well satisfied. It is good, then, to learn early in the game to avoid such errors by the simple trick shown in Fig. 23, where the centers of both the stencil and the surface to which it is to be applied are lined up.

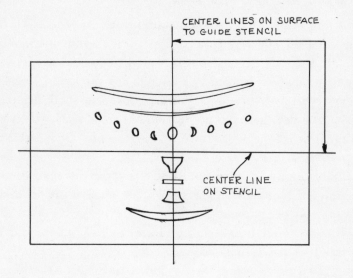

Fig. 23. How a stencil is centered upon the panel where it is to be applied.

For stencil work, metallic powders are seldom mixed with the liquid media intended for brush application. Occasionally a worker may be inclined to mix such powders with the liquids used with them (usually the so-called "banana oil") and to apply the mixture with a brush to some very small and intricate part of the

PLATE II

A rare Eli Terry wooden-works eight-day clock with typical stenciling and glass and face painting of the period between 1820 and 1830. *From the author's collection. Photograph by David E. Miller.)*

Examples of Pennsylvania Dutch Fraktur as practiced during the 1830s. The motifs are the same as those used during the last half of the eighteenth century. *(From the author's collection. Photograph by David E. Miller.)*

Fig. 24. Applying bronze powder to a surface with a piece of wool velvet.

stencil. This procedure, however, is not recommended for the stencil decoration of furniture or trays. Therefore, when we buy our metallic powders, we do not need to purchase the liquids with which such powders are mixed for brush application.

There are two methods by means of which the powders may be brought to the tacky varnished surface. The one preferred most often by the average worker makes use of wool velvet which has a very deep nap. A small piece of this material is wrapped around the index finger and folded over to hold it in place (see Fig. 24). This is dipped, perfectly dry, into the powder, which is thus conveyed from its container to the varnished surface showing through the stencil design.

Personally, I prefer a different kind of applicator because I have found that wool velvet has a tendency to pick up and hold too

Fig. 25. Crown-slat Hitchcock chair with pillow top and rush seat. (*Courtesy of Hitchcock Chair Co., Riverton, Conn.*)

Fig. 26. Turtle-slat Hitchcock chair with pillow top and rush seat. (*Courtesy of Hitchcock Chair Co., Riverton, Conn.*)

Fig. 27. Plain slat-back Hitchcock chair with rush seat. (*Courtesy of Hitchcock Chair Co., Riverton, Conn.*)

Fig. 28. Button-back Hitchcock chair with pillow top. (*Courtesy of Hitchcock Chair Co., Riverton, Conn.*)

much powder, thus increasing the danger that some of it will reach surfaces where it is not wanted.

In place of wool velvet, I use a small piece of chamois or suède. Even the finger cut from an old suède glove may be used. If suède is not available, then small pieces of chamois can usually be found at the local chain store for twenty-five or thirty cents. For greater convenience, this may be cut to shape, wrapped around the finger, and sewed. You may find, of course, that when either the velvet or the chamois is wrapped around the index finger, it is too bulky for the delicate work needed to produce good results in stenciling, and it might be well to experiment with both types of applicators on your test panels.

The correct amount of dry powder to be carried from the powder box to the stencil will depend upon that part of the stencil being treated—whether it is a large surface calling for a heavy, opaque application or a point where the powder is to be shaded or bled off. In any event, avoid pressing the finger down into the powder with too much pressure and bringing to your work a thickly packed mass of color. The greater the excess, the greater will be the danger of smearing or smudging. However, with the experience gained from a few test panels, you should be able to discover just about the correct amount of powder to be carried and to be applied to any particular part of your stencils.

SHADING STENCILS

It is to be presumed that you have seen at least one well-stenciled chair or other article bearing old stenciling. If so, you will have noted, no doubt, that only the very smallest components of such stencils were filled solid with gold, silver, or whatever color the design happened to be. Either one of two methods was used: The gold was filled in solid around the edges and bled or shaded off toward the center, or the center was made solid and the powder shaded off toward the edges. Much depended upon the nature of the design and upon where the leaf, apple, plum, peach, or melon of the design was located. Notice the shading in Fig. 28.

All good stencils involve good shading, and the modern worker who would best emulate the old work will do well to study and master, so far as possible, this business of shading. I know of no better way than the study of old work whenever the opportunity presents itself.

But there is a little more to the application of gold, bronze, or silver to stencils than the amount of powder to be carried by the applicator and the shading of the work. For one thing, we do not timidly dab the powder in place. Such application will only build up excessive amounts of powder poorly anchored in the tacky varnish and very grainy in appearance. What we seek, really, is just the reverse of these things—powder firmly anchored and a surface smooth and polished. If we dab the powder gently in place, we shall be in for trouble. It must be remembered at all times that our last coat of varnish has not been applied and that several protecting coats must be placed over freshly applied stencils immediately after the tackiness of the first coat, upon which the stencil was impressed, has dried—usually in about 24 hours. If we have badly anchored the metallic powder, the brush carrying the new varnish will quickly pick up the loose powder and carry it in unsightly streaks over the rest of the work. For this, alas, there is no remedy!

HOW TO POLISH APPLIED POWDER

As we gain experience in putting the gold or other powders in place on stencils, we shall discover that luster may be produced by gently polishing the powder as it is applied. Perhaps this will be more easily accomplished if it is done with chamois rather than with wool velvet.

Polishing is done either with a gentle circular motion or an oscillating, or back-and-forth, motion. Naturally, the pressure applied must not be so great as to scuff or roll the varnish. It is advisable to try this polishing on all the test panels, for it is polish that gives stencils their luster and brilliance.

TIME ELEMENT IN STENCILING

At this point I should like to emphasize again that the time element is important in stenciling and that good judgment will have to be exercised not only as to when to begin the application of the stenciling powder but also as to when to stop if you discover that the varnish has set up beyond the point where good adhesion is possible and you are faced with the necessity of applying another coat. The length of time will vary considerably, as might be expected with so many uncontrollable factors present. First and foremost, as we have mentioned before, there are the all-important elements of humidity and temperature. Other factors are the thickness with which the varnish is applied and the brand of varnish.

Some expert workers use a fast-setting varnish, like Valentine's Super-Valspar. This is a 4-hour mixture with a tacky period only long enough to accommodate the placing of a very small design, if it is being done by a slow-working beginner. Experts who work fast may find ample time even to put large, complicated stencils in place during the short time allowed.

Some experts who work slowly and insist upon plenty of time add a certain amount of linseed oil to their varnish to slow up the setting time. This is easily done, but it has disadvantages in that slowing up the drying time of the varnish also lengthens the time during which dust may settle and cling to the surface. Therefore, if the setting-up time of varnish is to be slowed up by the addition of an agent such as linseed oil, extra precaution against dust should be taken. Mixing ⅕ (by volume) of linseed oil to ⅘ of any of the conventional varnishes will extend the time for the tacky stage considerably.

That is about all that can helpfully be said about bronzing. The rest will have to come from experience, preferably gained on test panels, a procedure which cannot be too strongly recommended. If you by-pass the experience to be gained from the painting of trial panels, you may approach your first chair or other piece of furniture with a certain tension and fear of failure which will definitely militate against good results. One cannot stencil successfully in a dither.

USE OF COLORED PAINT

As in the nineteenth century, some modern stencilers prefer to work only with the metallic powders, while others like to add transparent or translucent colors to their flowers or fruits after the metallic powders have been applied in stencil form. There can be no question about it, the cautious addition of color will do something for a stencil if it is applied skillfully. Again the advisability of practice work on panels is obvious. And it is understood, of course, that the color is put on the stencils *after* they have been covered with a coat of the kind of varnish that will eventually be used as a finish for the whole chair or article to be decorated.

These color applications are referred to as "color overtones." Skillfully applied, they add warmth and charm to any piece of work. As an example, let us take a bunch of grapes stenciled in light gold and given an overtone of Prussian blue, one of the artist's oil colors that are partially transparent. When the blue is applied over the gold grapes, part of the gold shows through. This would not be the case, however, if an opaque artist's color were used; it would completely blanket the gold underneath. Since many artist's colors in oil are opaque, it is well to have before us the modest list of transparent artist's colors that can be used over stencils. They are: alizarin red or crimson, Prussian blue, gamboge or yellow lake, verdigris, and mauve. Although limited, the list provides colors that can be used on a wide variety of stencils. For instance, leaves treated with green (verdigris) will prove to be most attractive.

Oil colors are not applied directly as they come from the collapsible tubes in which they are purchased. In this condition they will be anything but transparent, and it will also take them a very long time to harden enough so as to eliminate the possibility of trouble when varnish is placed over them. Such colors must be mixed with varnish before they are applied. To prepare our colored varnish, we put a small amount of turpentine in a small dish and add three times that amount of varnish—the same varnish we shall use later to cover the ·piece of furniture. To this mixture we add enough color from the tube to produce the shade we want. Here, again, a bit of experience in finishing test panels will give us guidance in color mixing. We must be careful to add only very small amounts at a time, for if there is too much color in our mixture, nothing can be done about it. On the other hand, if there is too little, we can keep adding small amounts and making trial brushouts on a piece of varnished paper until we arrive at the correct amount.

The color is applied with a small camel's-hair brush, and the density of the paint should follow the density and bleeding off of the gold or whatever metallic powder was used. In short, we do not simply fill in a leaf, a grape, or an apple with color but shade the color to correspond with the dark-to-light shading of the stencil design.

After colors have been applied, we must be sure they are thoroughly dry before we put on an overcoating of varnish. If the colors have not hardened properly, the varnish will pick up some of the color and smear it, thereby spoiling all your work up to that point. If this should happen to a mild extent, a careful swabbing with clean cotton moistened with turpentine may help.

COMPOSITE STENCILS

Thus far we have said very little about multiple-unit, or composite, stencils. While simple stencil patterns may be applied with a single-piece stencil, more complicated designs must be applied with two or more stencils. Involved patterns may require as many as eight or ten separate stencils, each one applied separately and in the proper sequence.

Let us take as an example a stencil design involving a compote of fruit. The compote holds melons, plums, peaches, grapes.

Fig. 29. Two of the more simple stencils of the floral and fruit types used on the cheaper chairs during the 1830s.

and apples, together with leaves of one or more of these fruits. If we attempted to cut a single stencil containing all these components, the stencil would be too complicated and fragile for practical use. Also, it would produce the same pattern each time it was used, whereas a multipiece, or composite, stencil with a separate cutout for each piece of fruit makes a variety of patterns possible. Each time you use such a series of stencils, you can produce a different pattern; on one occasion a bunch of grapes droops off one side of the compote, and on another occasion it droops off the opposite side.

In Fig. 30 we see the form taken by the various stencils used to make up a compote of fruit. Not one, but several, stencils are used for such things as peaches, grapes, and leaves. We must have a stencil not only for a complete grape and a complete peach but also one for a half grape and a half peach. Thus we supply ourselves with a single composite stencil and with the possibility of an infinite variety of patterns. Each time the stencil is used a wholly new pattern can be devised with the various components.

CARE OF STENCILS

The proper care of stencils is most important. After they have been used, they should be wiped off with a clean cloth moistened

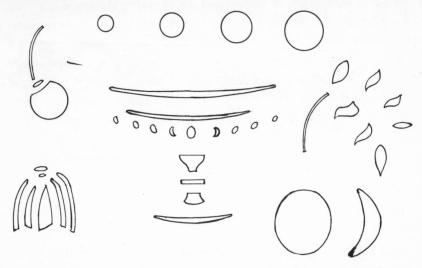

Fig. 30. The simple components of a fruit-and-compote stencil.

Fig. 31. One way in which the stencil components shown in Fig. 30 may be applied. Many arrangements of the same set of stencils may be used.

with a solvent such as those used for cleaning paintbrushes. We must be careful, however, not to expose our skin to these solvents any more than necessary because they quickly dissolve out all surface oil and fat.

After the stencils have been wiped clean and dustless, they should be stored carefully between waxed paper, which will keep them clean and flat for the time when they will be used again.

CHAPTER VIII

Striping, Varnishing, and Antiquing

ALTHOUGH striping is not to be found to any extent on other articles of stenciled furniture, it was universally used on seats of all types of chairs—side chairs, kitchen chairs, Boston rockers, and benches. Therefore, if we are to reproduce faithfully the decoration of old fancy chairs, the reproduction must include striping in conventional forms. Figure 32 shows a variety of striped patterns used on old chairs.

Striping may be done with gold, bronze, silver, copper, or any of the japan colors. The various shades of gold and bronze along with silver (really aluminum) are employed successfully only on a black background.

Painting stripes evenly is admittedly difficult, but with practice and with a steady hand there is little reason why you cannot do a really presentable job.

When we were ready to take up stenciling, I advised the making of a number of test panels before starting actual work on a chair. We shall not need to use trial panels for striping practice, but we should experiment on the edge of an old board or other surface, using any kind of paint.

Striping brushes can be purchased at well-stocked paint stores, or they can be made at home. You should have at least two brushes, one for very fine striping and one for heavy striping. The brush for the latter use need be nothing more difficult to find than a very small, good-quality artist's brush. Indeed, an excellent striping brush for fine lines can be made from a long-bristled artist's brush by thinning out some of the bristles with a small pair of

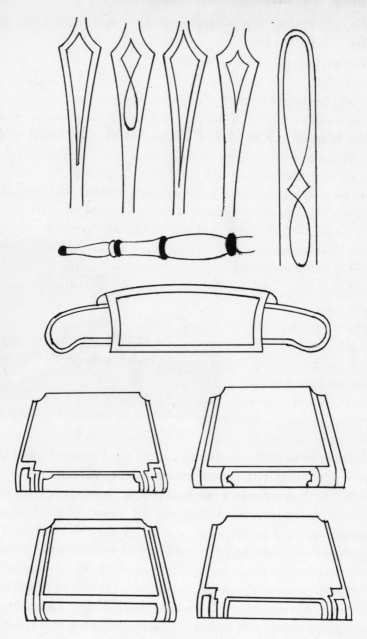

Fig. 32. Examples of the variations in striping on chair seats, legs, and slats. The gold bands on the chair legs were rarely carried all the way around.

scissors, the cutting being done near the ferrule that holds the bristles.

Whether you purchase your brushes or make them yourself, the technique of using them will be the same; the brush in all cases will be held between the fingers as illustrated in Fig. 33. Of course, this method of holding the brush is used only when a stripe is to be produced that will run perfectly parallel to an edge. When curlicues, loops, and scrolls are to be painted, other methods of brush holding will have to be adopted.

The perfect stripes that were produced by skilled coach painters

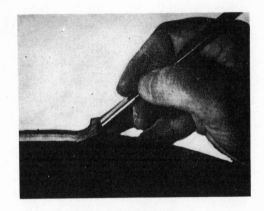

Fig. 33. The proper way to hold a striping brush when working on an edge. The brush is held with the thumb, index and third fingers, while the fourth finger is placed on the edge of the article to be striped, and this serves as a guide when the brush is moved along.

of old were of uniform width throughout their entire length, and they were painted with great speed and skill. Not only the width but also the straightness was precise. This was possible because the coach painters learned to move the painting hand in one dimension only. Once the hand was set to paint as illustrated in Fig. 33, and once it began to move, there was no wobble from side to side and no wavering up and down. The hand was kept at a precise level above the stripe. It will be readily understood that if the hand holding the brush wavers up and down, the brush will move up and down, and this will cause the hairs in the brush to spread and contract with the motion of the hand. The brush will spread slightly when the hand comes down ever so little, and the reverse will happen when the hand goes up. The result will be a stripe of varying width.

STRIPING WITH MASKING TAPE

For those who do not relish the thought of gaining proficiency with a striping brush, there is the possibility of using stencils and masking tape. Where a stripe is to be made parallel to an edge, masking tape can be put on in the manner illustrated in Fig. 34, and the line can be painted with an ordinary artist's brush. Even scrolls and curlicues can be produced in the same manner. The professional objection to this procedure, however, is based upon artistic grounds; the resulting stripes will be far too mechanically perfect. There can be no doubt that a stripe produced by the unaided hand is easily distinguished from those produced by a stencil or by the use of masking tape.

A study of the striping on old chairs reveals that some lines are narrow and delicate while others are relatively wide. Some are

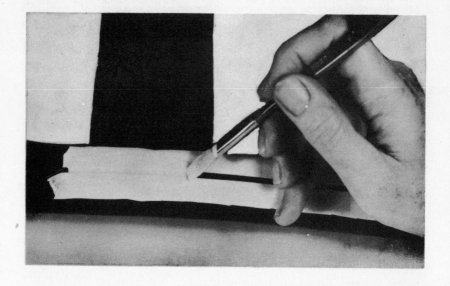

Fig. 34. How parallel strips of ordinary masking tape are used for striping on chair posts.

about ⅛ inch from the edge, and others are more than that. In a few cases, we note that instead of stripes, there is a gold edge only (Fig. 35), which is much more easily produced with a striping brush or other small brush than is a single line with black on either side of it.

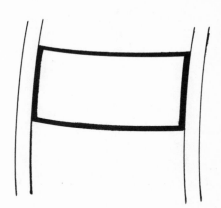

Fig. 35. Striping that goes over the edge of chair slats and top rails was commonly used back in the 1820s and 1830s.

Further study of old chairs also reveals the application of gold or bronze to the turned bands on the legs, rungs, or stretchers and on certain top rails of the pillow-back type. It should be noted, however, that the old decorators never carried the application of bronze in such spots to completion. The bronze stripe was not extended all the way around the turnings, the backs of them being left uncovered for the simple reason that a person standing in front of the chair would never notice the absence of the finishing touch. Of course, if the modern worker is going to produce authentic decorations, he, too, will neglect to apply the bronze all the way around.

STRIPING WITH YELLOW PAINT

Another interesting fact brought to light by a study of old chairs is that the relatively heavy lines were produced with bronze paint, whereas the very fine and delicate ones were produced with yellow paint. From a practical point of view, this procedure should be followed today. Because of the tendency of bronze or gold paint to spread after being applied, it is much more difficult to produce a fine line with it than with yellow paint.

To mix yellow paint for fine lines, we place a daub or two of opaque chrome yellow and a drop or two of turpentine in a tiny dish or metal bottle cap. To this we add a bit of yellow ocher and a little burnt umber, mixing all three together until we get a mustardlike color. This mustard shade, however, will turn to a more pronounced yellow when it is applied to a black surface. To this mixture we add 24-hour clear varnish until we have the right consistency. A few test applications should be made on a black surface as a color check. If the color is not the correct shade of rather brilliant yellow, we should add a little more chrome yellow.

It may be necessary to experiment a bit until we get the knack of creating just the right shade. Especially will it be necessary not to add so much varnish as to give the yellow a greenish cast after it has been applied. This can be corrected by the addition of still more yellow. If the mixture is too thick to flow well on application, a few drops of tincture of benzoin will produce a temporary liquidity which will make application much easier with no danger of altering the color.

STRIPING WITH GOLD

The gold paint for wide striping is produced by mixing the metallic powder with the same kind of varnish as described above. The addition of the powder to the varnish should cease when the mixture becomes thick enough to cover a black surface with no black showing through. It will be well to add powder cautiously to the varnish and to test frequently until the proper consistency has been reached. Again, if the mixture is a little too thick to flow easily, tincture of benzoin may be added to aid application. Tincture of benzoin may also be used to restore liquidity if we find it necessary to leave our striping mixtures unused until they become too thick for application.

The striping brush is dipped freely into the paint mixture, and the excess is scraped off on the edge of the container. Actually the brush should be as full of paint as it can be without danger of dripping. The less paint we carry to the spot where we are going to make the stripe, the more often we shall have to go back and pick up where we left off. This makes for a broken, wavy line—at least until we become far more skillful than we can possibly be in the beginning.

Any piece of furniture newly decorated with bronze or gold stencils and striped with bright yellow will appear very new and shiny at first. It will not have an antique look. We must remember, however, that the old chairs probably appeared just as new when they came forth from the Hitchcock and other factories 125 years ago. Our newly decorated chairs may not appear to be authentic because they lack the signs of age; but unless they are exceptionally gaudy, that is the way I suggest they be left. It will not be long—a few years at the most—before the varnish will darken noticeably and tone down the brightness of the decorations. Clear varnish has a tendency to turn brown with age.

ANTIQUE FINISH

Some refinishers of old stenciled furniture prefer to establish a synthetic antiquity by applying colored varnish to produce an antique brown. The trouble is that in a few years the antique effect becomes antique with a vengeance, because of the brown oil color that was added to the varnish and the natural darkening of the varnish itself. After several years the effect may be far too pronounced. Therefore, if antiquing is to be done with varnish, we must guard against using colors that are too deep in the first place, remembering that within a relatively short time we shall have a natural change of color in the varnish.

This decision on antiquing must be left to the best judgment of the reader—not only as to whether or not he will do it but as to the degree of tone to use if he does decide to do it. Following are complete instructions for antiquing.

Antiquing starts after the stenciling and striping have been done and have been given some 48 hours to dry. First we mix a small amount of burnt umber, which is a reddish-brown, with a small amount of turpentine and pour the color into enough varnish to cover the chair twice. We use ordinary Valentine's varnish, either the 4-hour or the 24-hour variety. What we seek is not a deep brown but just an off shade of brown. If, after applying a single coat, we decide that the color is not quite dark enough, we simply add another coat, but not before the first coat has had 24 hours in which to dry.

The second or third coat of varnish, as the case may be, should be clear, as it comes from the can, because this final coat is the one that is rubbed down with crude oil and pumice. The varnish should be given 48 hours to set before the rubbing begins.

USE OF PUMICE

Crude oil, usually available at any drugstore, is mixed with pumice powder to produce a mixture of creamlike consistency. This is applied to the chair with a piece of an old felt hat and is worked over small areas with only moderate pressure. If too great pressure is used, the pumice will cut far too fast. At least we should use light pressure in the beginning until we get the "feel" of this sort of operation.

We must at all times be careful in using pumice near edges. Because of the tendency to increase pressure on edges, there is a real danger of cutting through the varnish at such points, even though we may think we are not bearing down any harder here than on flat surfaces.

We may find it convenient to rub the rungs or stretchers and legs with an old nylon stocking rather than a piece of felt. This procedure is heartily recommended. The stocking is applied in the same manner as a cloth in shining shoes.

This rubbing is done for the sole purpose of relieving the varnish of its high gloss, not to improve the smoothness of the surface. If the varnish has been put on under good dust-free conditions, there will be no need to improve its smoothness.

After the rubbing has been completed, it will be necessary to wash off the residue of oil and pumice with warm water and a bit of Ivory soap. A good wax furniture polish, thinly applied after the chair has dried, should give the job a fine finished appearance.

CHAPTER IX

Painting Tin Trays

TRAY PAINTING or stenciling can be a most satisfying hobby, what with the many motifs available, the ease with which they can be painted, and the practical value of the finished article. Properly stenciled or painted, trays will hold their charm and antique luster for years and may even become family heirlooms.

There are a number of ways in which trays may be finished, some of them much shorter than others. The short cut, however, is not the method for the true hobbyist who wants his or her handicraft to represent the best practice and to produce not only the greatest possible beauty but the greatest longevity. Often it is not so much artistic skill as patience that produces the most beautiful trays.

Those about to take up this fascinating hobby will first want to know where to obtain suitable trays of various shapes and sizes. One of the best sources is the auction. Rarely do the furnishings of any but the most recently established households fail to bring forth a tin tray of some sort—and it is the so-called "tin tray" that is used for the painting and stenciling. Actually, these trays, old or modern, are not tin; they are thin sheet iron plated with tin to prevent corrosion. Such tin plating is done by the hot-dip method; that is, the sheet iron is dipped into molten tin.

FINDING OLD TRAYS

Although most of my own collection of tin trays have come from country and city auctions, this is not, of course, the only source. Good antique trays may be found at auctions, but not at reasonable prices unless they are finished in plain black japan. If they possess

74

their original decorative stencils in good condition, and if members of the antique-collecting fraternity are about, some fancy bidding will result. I have seen many such trays go for prices between twenty and thirty-five dollars. On the other hand, plain trays without decoration of any sort may often be bought for a few cents. You do not need to worry about the damage to the finish because it must all be removed anyway. What you must be very fussy about, however, is damage caused by bending or dents. Trays harmed in this manner are not worth lugging home—and this caution comes from one considered to be fairly handy with tools who has tried desperately on a number of occasions to eliminate such damage. Always the little bulge or the tiny tell-tale dimples remain.

Trays decorated in modern and crudely duplicated old designs can be bought in the chain stores, though usually in limited shapes and sizes—oval, round, and oblong. However, if the hobbyist finds such a supply and if the shapes suit him or her, they should be purchased. The enamel and designs can be readily removed, as will be described later.

More professional sources of supply will have to be found for the unusual shapes such as the Chippendale, Queen Anne, etc. These trays come in a variety of sizes and in two conditions—either raw metal or metal sprayed with black. Prices may range from seven dollars for the very large sizes (22 by 29 inches) to thirty-five cents for the 6- by 8-inch size. Some of the shapes in which blank trays are supplied to the trade are shown in Fig. 36. These are reproduction shapes, all of them also available in genuinely old trays.

The next step, unless you have obtained trays of raw metal, is to remove the old or new finish. All old finishes quickly respond to any of the modern paint and varnish removers. But here again a warning should be posted. All such removers contain powerful solvents that possess two extremely dangerous hazards—injury to eyesight and fire. Also, the vapors from these solvents are highly toxic, more so for some people than for others. Therefore they

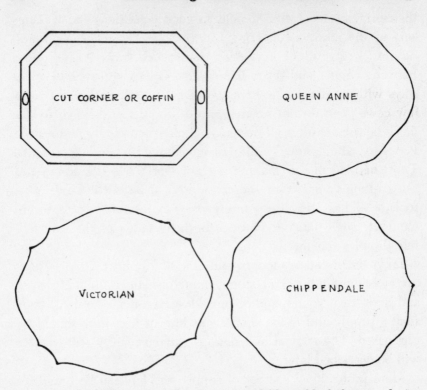

Fig. 36. The different tray shapes now available in blank form ready for painting. They are usually sold through art stores or hobby shops.

should be used only with the windows open or, preferably, out of doors.

REMOVING OLD FINISH

The paint or varnish remover is simply flooded on (one surface at a time) with an old paintbrush and then allowed to stand for the time specified on the can, which is usually not more than ten minutes. Old coarse rags may be used to brush the old varnish, japan, or paint away. Rarely does the first application of the remover completely soften the covering; sometimes several applications will be needed. The last application is followed by a good going-over with coarse steel wool, then an energetic rubbing with

Fig. 37. Hand-painted, stenciled-border tray of the so-called "Chippendale shape." (*Courtesy of the Society for the Preservation of New England Antiquities.*)

Fig. 38. Another example of an old Chippendale hand-painted tray. (*Courtesy of the Society for the Preservation of New England Antiquities.*)

fine steel wool, which should remove the last vestige of the painted surface.

CLEANING TRAYS

All modern paint removers contain a certain amount of wax, which is intended for the protection of the wood fibers from which paint or varnish is to be removed. This wax residue can raise hob on a tray unless it is completely removed. Removal of the wax can be greatly facilitated by wiping the tray with a rag soaked in turpentine and then with a rag soaked in carbon tetrachloride. A good scrubbing in hot soapy water or detergent should follow. After that, the water-break test should be tried (see page 80). If the water film is consistently broken, then further washing in warm soapy water or detergent should be assisted by the energetic use of a clean stiff brush. A surface free of water breaks must be established.

If you should find a painted surface that does not respond readily to the above treatment, a hot lye bath will probably turn the trick. I hesitate to recommend the use of this chemical, which is dangerously corrosive to the skin, but the following directions are provided if the worker wishes to take the chances involved.

A full can of ordinary lye is added to 3 or 4 gallons of hot water, which is stirred until the lye is thoroughly dissolved. The piece or pieces to be cleaned are immersed in the solution, and then the container, which may be a galvanized-metal washtub or trash can, is placed over a fire and permitted to boil slowly for a half to three quarters of an hour. The tinware is then removed and is given a complete and thorough rinsing, after which it should be bright and clean. (Another warning: Before using lye, you should understand the extremely harsh action of a hot lye solution on the flesh and should be extremely careful not to splash it on the skin or in the eyes. The wearing of glasses or goggles is advised.)

If you have a raw-metal tray, you simply wash it thoroughly with a mild soap and plenty of suds; then rinse it in plenty of clean water, handling it thereafter with clean cotton gloves that are used only for this purpose. The best way to keep them clean and free of dust is to place them in a paper bag between usings. The tray may be placed underneath a cardboard carton while drying. As a matter of fact, trays in the various states of finish must all be kept underneath a clean carton until drying is beyond the stage at which the air-borne dust particles, bane of all finishers, will do harm. Any dust particle, even though invisible to the eye, can cause an easily seen pimple on a wet surface because of the effects of capillarity.

Many expert tray painters make good use of a little device long since known to the painting fraternity as a "tack rag." This rag has a tacky surface that is capable of picking up fine particles of metal and dust without leaving any behind. A tack rag is useful, I feel, so long as it is not used beyond its capacity to hold dirt. They are cheap enough so that you can keep a fresh one near by and a clean one in use.

Not all trays are dipped in tin as carefully as they should be, and this may be true of some trays supplied in raw condition. Often the tin deposit is a trifle bumpy. In such cases, the surface should be treated first with coarse steel wool and then with fine steel wool. The worker should try to preserve the tin plate wherever possible, but a tiny break-through here and there will do no harm. After a cleaning of this kind the surface should be smoother. Superfine particles of metal left by this smoothing process may be flushed away under a water faucet. The tray is then further cleaned in a soapy solution. There is no reason, however, why this degreasing or cleaning cannot be accomplished with one of the modern detergents if the worker so desires.

To the impatient person, all this careful preparation may seem petty and irksome, but it is necessary if you hope to achieve lasting and beautiful results. In every case your aim is to achieve a flawless antique surface full of charm and subtlety, and it can be achieved only by painstaking attention to every detail that has thus far been discussed. There are no short cuts to the perfect job.

Careless stripping and cleaning, for example, ruin a work that might otherwise last for a century. Furthermore, this can ruin it quickly—long before the hobbyist has received his full reward in the joy of contemplating his handiwork and showing it with justifiable pride to his friends. It cannot be too strongly emphasized that the japanned or enameled surfaces over which you will place decorations must be established on a scrupulously clean metal surface to prevent immediate blistering or subsequent peeling.

After a tray has been cleaned, even the grease left by a finger touch should be avoided, not only on the clean metal but also on japanned, varnished, or enameled surfaces. As mentioned earlier, once trays have been stripped and cleaned, they should be handled with clean cotton gloves. This advice holds also for handling between each successive layer of the carefully established surface produced by applications of enamel or japan. Even a blank tray received from a hobby-supply house should be washed carefully. Such a tray was undoubtedly cut out on a punch press from a large, oil-covered sheet of tin plate, and it is a sure bet that its surface still bears a microscopic film of oil invisible to the eye. Grease in any form, animal or vegetable, can be fatal to the results.

In getting rid of grease, we might take a tip from the electroplater, who must also fight grease if his plating is not to peel. He has a quick test for the presence of grease on clean metal surfaces. The article is simply dipped in freshly drawn water and is then examined for what the electroplater calls "water breaks." After the article is withdrawn from the clean water bath, it should be covered completely with a thin, even film of water. This film, however, will be broken where grease in any form remains, because the water will not adhere to such surfaces.

ELIMINATING RUST

Rust, like dirt, is a vicious enemy of the tray painter. Not the slightest vestige of rust should ever be allowed to remain before the first coat of paint is applied. Rust is a curious and mystifying disease of iron and steel, which to this day is not thoroughly understood by metallurgists. It may be called a malignancy of iron and steel, capable of spreading once it has started. If, after a raw metal tray has been smoothed, cleaned, and dried, a tiny speck of rust is found, it should be carefully wiped away with fine steel wool, and the metal dust carefully blown away from the spot.

Oftentimes this battle against rust may be helped by a commercial preparation to be found in most hardware stores. It is called Rusticide. When applied as directed, this substance greatly facilitates the removal of rust.

When old trays are being prepared for refinishing, one should watch for excessive corrosion after the old finish has been removed. By excessive corrosion I mean the kind that destroys surfaces to such a degree that no amount of treatment with fine emery cloth followed by steel wool will restore the surface to its original smoothness. It is the nature of both enamel and japan that even four or five applications will not obliterate the surface irregularities so created. A better course would be to use such trays for practice and experimentation.

Now, with your tray perfectly clean, the covering procedure is as follows:

It would be easy, of course, to slap on two or three coats of black japan or other colors and then to begin to paint the design. This would cut down finishing and painting time by several hundred per cent, but the job would not be good. Far from it. A better idea is to plan to spend several weeks preparing the background, painting the design, and varnishing.

But first, here are instructions for handling wet trays. Inasmuch as both top and bottom surfaces of each tray are to be painted and varnished a number of times, the working time would be doubled if the worker painted only one surface and then allowed the usual 24 hours for drying before painting the other side.

I have overcome this problem with the simple gadget illustrated in Fig. 39. Only one needs to be made for trays of all sizes. It is simply a sharp, four-pointed rest upon which the wet bottoms of trays may be placed. This admittedly leaves small marks on the bottoms of finished trays, but if the priming coats are as thin as they should be and this surface is gradually built up, the marks will be hardly noticeable. Of course, if heavy coats of japan or dull black are applied, very heavy marks will be left.

This method of drying requires that the japan, or whatever is being used, be placed on the bottom of the tray first, with two spots left uncovered for lifting, as illustrated in Fig. 39. This done, the tray is slid over the edge of the worktable, one end at a time, and then lifted at the unpainted spots. It is placed top-side-up on the four sharpened points, and the neglected spots on the bottom are then painted immediately from beneath. No great time should elapse between these operations; otherwise the bottom paint will become tacky before the dry spots are covered.

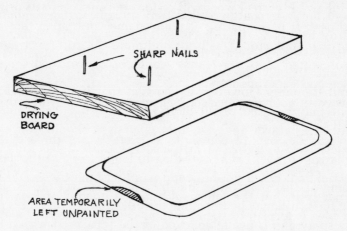

Fig. 39. A simple homemade holding device for drying freshly painted trays. Small unpainted portions are left on the bottom at each end of the tray for lifting.

PRODUCING THAT "OLD LOOK"

Before we begin to paint, let us assume that the hobbyist wishes to achieve only the finest possible results and that he wants his finished trays not only to appear as professional as possible but also to have an "old look." There are various methods of finishing trays, but I feel that there is only one way to produce the fine, mellow appearance that is so desirable. It should be understood that the most satisfactory results are not produced by the quality of the painting alone. The world's best artists could paint flowers or fruit on trays, and the most skillful stencilers could decorate them with borders, without producing the best results. Much would depend on the quality of the prime surface upon which they worked and also on the varnished surface that was placed over their work. The proper result is that of a soft, slightly worn enameled surface with a general antique effect. One must have felt and seen such a surface to know it.

USE OF RED PRIMER

There is an undercoating called "red primer" that is available at all hardware stores. It has been used for many years on metal and was, indeed, developed for this purpose alone. It is not satisfactory for wood. Usually this primer can be applied directly to trays without thinning. However, if you feel that it is too thick, turpentine may be used to cut it. If you brush it on, you must be careful to establish an even, thin coat. Nor should you expect opaque coverage with the first coat. Because it has very little body, it has a tendency to weep on the tray edges. If there is weeping at this point after the tray has been set on its drying stand, the brush may be run along the edge to take up excess paint.

If a spray gun is available, even of the type used with a home vacuum cleaner, it may be used. For this kind of application, use a clip and hang the tray from a clothesline. You do not need to worry about the unpainted spot left by the clip because the clip is moved to the other end when the second coat is put on.

USING STEEL WOOL

After the first coat of red primer has been allowed to dry for 24 hours, it should be treated with the fine steel wool. The treatment is light, not heavy. Hard pressure and lengthy rubbing will remove too much of the primer.

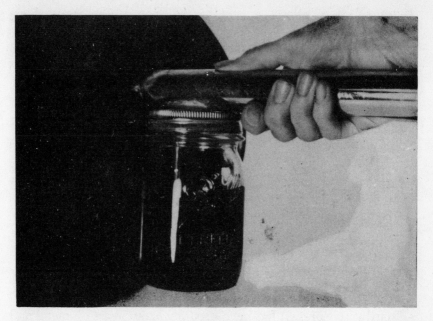

Fig. 40. Using the spraying attachment of a home vacuum cleaner for applying thin enamel or asphalt paint to a tray.

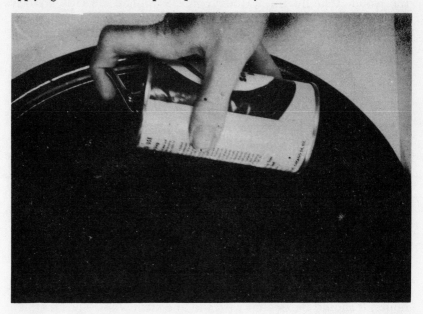

Fig. 41. Using one of the new spray cans of enamel for building up several thin coats on a metal tray.

A note of caution here in connection with the use of steel wool: If it is carelessly employed, tiny slivers of steel may get into the skin and flesh of your hand and cause trouble if you are subject to infections. This difficulty can be prevented by handling the wool with a small piece of soft chamois between it and the fingers.

After the primer has been treated with the steel wool, it should be wiped off with the tack cloth and another coat of primer applied in exactly the same manner. This, too, is given a steel-wool "once-over" and wiped with the tack pad. If, with the second coat, you have a solid, dull red surface unbroken by thin off-color streaks, you are ready to proceed. On the other hand, if the surface is broken and streaky, another coat of primer should be applied. I have found that the several brands of metal primers differ so much in consistency that it is difficult to set a two-coat priming as the final answer. It may or it may not be. I might add here that these red primers are supposed to prevent corrosion through rust.

DRYING WITHOUT DUST

To prepare for the next step, we must have a perfectly clean carton large enough to be placed over the wet tray after each coat of black japan is applied. Before the carton is used, it should be inverted and the bottom slapped to dislodge any dust that might be on the inside surfaces. We should also take the additional precaution of wiping the inside surfaces with a clean, moist cloth.

The precautions mentioned should not be brushed aside, for in a very large measure the proper finishing of trays is a constant fight against air-borne dust. Many an otherwise beautifully painted tray has been given a bad case of smallpox by careless protection against dust. And let no one, no matter how skillful he may be, think that such particles can be removed by even the most dexterous application of pumice, rotten stone, fine sandpaper, or steel wool. *It cannot be done!*

However much you wish to keep dust out with the inverted carton placed over the wet tray, some circulation of air will be necessary if the tray is to dry within a reasonable time. The best way to allow for circulation is to scallop the edge of the carton so that when it is inverted over the wet tray, air will not be cut off.

But drying is not the only point at which dust may be picked up. It can come from clothing, from agitation on the bench, from a dirty brush, etc. Perhaps we can take a few hints from the old coach painters, who always wet the room down and sometimes worked naked when the last finishing coats were put in place. To minimize the danger of dust at the final stage, clothing on the upper portion of the body should be freshly laundered, if possible, and the bench and the area near where the work is to be done should be wiped off with a damp cloth.

The brush, more than anything else, may bring dust to the tray. Only the very best varnish brushes should be used, 1 or 1½ inches in width. If a brush does not have a paper bag over its bristles when it is purchased, it should be carefully rinsed out in turpentine before it is used.

It would be preferable that no finishing be attempted if the worker must economize by trying to revive an old paintbrush with a brush cleaner. It is almost impossible to dislodge small particles of dried paint from the heels of such brushes, and they will constantly be working themselves down from above.

A word about brush care is also pertinent at this point. Brushes must not only be dust-free when they are placed in service, but they must be kept that way. To keep them that way, the simple arrangement shown in Fig. 22 is employed, with turpentine or kerosene as the liquid. With turpentine, the brush need only be swished dry when it is ready for use. A kerosene-soaked brush will have to be soaked in turpentine and swished out several times before it is to be used.

APPLYING FINISHING COATS

The priming coats in place, the tray is ready for the black. Two or three coats of a mixture of Ivory Black Drop in japan are put on either by spraying or with a scrupulously clean varnish brush. The various coats should be separated by a 24-hour drying period.

PLATE III

Good examples of modern brush-stroke painting on tinware articles. Both motifs and technique are borrowed from the 1830s. *(Courtesy of Katherine Worden. Photograph by David E. Miller.)*

If for any reason the japan is not thin enough for spray application, it may readily be thinned with turpentine. If you overshoot the mark in thinning it, no great harm will be done. The worst that can happen is that an extra coat may be needed. Ordinarily only two coats are needed over the red primer.

A word about bubbles may be in order here. Many painters are troubled with them when applying japan and varnish. Bubbles result when these liquids are shaken in the can or stirred too violently, thus mixing air with the liquids. Japans and varnishes with color in them should be stirred gently, and if bubbles appear, they should be allowed to settle out.

As in the case of the primer, the tray is set away to dry for at least 24 hours after receiving the first coat of japan. At the end of this period its whole surface, top and bottom, is gently gone over with fine steel wool. Pressure should be just enough to gray the black surface slightly, and this operation is followed promptly with the tack pad to pick up the slight dust that will be produced by the use of the steel wool.

Another coat of japan is then put on by the same method, and this is also followed by the application of steel wool. The work is now ready for the base of varnish, and this varnish must have qualities beyond that of merely being good. Above all, the varnish should be able to stand up under the abuse to which it may be subjected. It is to be remembered that trays are used to serve both alcoholic and nonalcoholic drinks and that their surfaces may be exposed to both acid and alkaline liquids.

APPLYING VARNISH

Thus far I have found nothing superior to Valentine's Valspar for the several varnish coats for trays. Valspar may be used from the first coat to the last, but the undercoats, such as the one placed directly over the japan, may be another Valentine product called Sheraton, which is a quick-rubbing varnish, excellent for the building up of fine surfaces. If this is used in the undercoatings, the Valspar may be used for the finishing coats.

After the application of the first coat of either Sheraton or Valspar varnish over the japan, and after it has dried for 24 hours (or more if the atmosphere is especially humid), you will be ready to put on the prepared design.

APPLYING DESIGN

In the application of stencils, the worker sometimes discovers, after he has removed the stencil, that he has forgotten to apply the bronze, gilt, or silver to a certain part. Considerable fussing and trouble will result from trying to replace the stencil in its original position for proper registration. All such inconvenience may be eliminated, however, by following the procedure illustrated in Fig. 42. Center lines, both vertical and horizontal, are made on both the tray and the stencil, the lines on the tray being made with a soapstone pencil, which may be purchased at well-stocked hardware stores or paint shops. When the stencil is placed on the tray, the center lines should be aligned. Thus the worker is assured not only that he has his design in the exact center of the tray in the first place, but that he may put it back in exactly the same place if necessary.

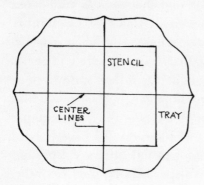

Fig. 42. A method for ensuring that the stencil will be placed in the exact center of a tray. The marks on the tray may be made with a soapstone pencil.

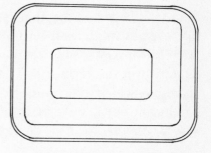

Fig. 43. How the striping may be installed on plain oblong trays. The center panel may be expanded or contracted to encompass the main motif.

The stencil is held to the surface of the tray with masking tape—just enough to hold the stencil firmly. The tape should not be pressed in place too firmly nor left for a long period of time.

If a hand-painted design instead of a stencil is to be used on a tray, a slightly different procedure is required. The mechanics of tracing designs on trays is simple enough if the following directions are observed with some degree of caution.

One method employs a fine white powder called "lithopone," which is used to coat the design on tracing paper of the type employed by draftsmen. Excessive powder, which is very light and fluffy, will have to be removed before the transfer paper is laid on the tray.

Perhaps the second method (which is described below) is more to be recommended for the beginner, because it eliminates the necessity for obtaining lithopone powder, sometimes difficult to find, and also eliminates the rather complicated preparation for this transfer method.

The second method simply makes use of canary-colored transfer paper if the design is to be traced on a black or dark surface. If the design is to be traced on an old-ivory or other light surface (all trays are not finished in black japan), ordinary graphite paper or carbon paper may be used. In any case, small pieces of either masking tape or Scotch tape are used to hold the tracing paper to the tray until the design is transferred.

It is assumed that the design decided upon has already been traced from its source onto a piece of thin tracing paper, such as that used by draftsmen. This is then placed over the transfer paper attached to the tray and the lines are followed with a sharp, hard pencil point. Every detail should be carefully covered.

ANTIQUING TRAYS

More will be said about the actual painting in Chapter X. It is now assumed that the design has either been painted in or stenciled in, as the case may be, and that the worker is ready to apply the finishing coats. This is the step which produces good trays with century-old appearance. Indeed, it is in the final finishing of trays that the worker will discover whether he is a true hobbyist or whether tray finishing is just a passing fancy, for patience, and plenty of it, will be required.

Naturally, before the first of the protecting coats of varnish is applied, you must make sure that you will not run into the greatest disaster that can befall a tray refinisher—not having your stencil or floral decorations dry enough before the first varnish coat is applied. It is sad, indeed, to see long hours of preparation ruined when the first brush strokes pick up some of the bronze powder or oil paint and smear it across the tray. The answer is simple enough: *plenty of drying time!* Fifty to sixty hours may not be too much.

The varnished surface is built up carefully, layer by layer, with 24-hour periods of drying and rubbing between layers. Valentine's Sheraton brand of varnish is recommended for all but the last layer, which should be Valspar because of its previously mentioned resistance to alcohol, etc. Sheraton varnish responds nicely to the rubbing down required between coats.

The worker seeks the finest possible surface, and this requires that the varnish be applied smoothly. To achieve this the varnish should not be too thick or at too low a temperature. All varnishes become more fluid when gently warmed. Greater fluidity means easier and more uniform application. The can containing the varnish may be set in a pan filled with hot water. Within a few minutes the heat will penetrate into the varnish, and it will be ready for use. In no case should the varnish be heated on a gas stove. Nor should the varnish can be shaken before it is opened, if air bubbles are to be avoided.

A soft, clean varnish brush is used, with the usual precautions against weeping and excessive amounts of varnish on the beading and edges. Naturally, the drying rack previously described is used. It will be possible to apply a more even coat of varnish if the tray is gently warmed in an open gas-stove oven before the varnish is applied. What is said concerning the application of this first coat will hold for all following coats.

The room in which the finishing coats are applied should be as free from dust as possible, and all drying should be done under the carton previously mentioned. Cold rooms should be avoided as well as damp places. For instance, a cellar in the summertime is a bad place for drying trays. In the winter, with the furnace in operation, a cellar may be all right so long as the temperature does not fall much below 70 degrees. We also try to avoid a drying room where people are constantly moving about.

If Sheraton varnish is used, 24 hours of drying under favorable conditions will be sufficient for each of the five coats that will be needed. This means that it will be practically a week before you will be ready for the last coat of Valspar.

After the first coat has dried for 24 hours, the tray is removed from under the carton and gently treated to a rubbing on both sides with the finest steel wool. All that is needed here is to produce a slightly dull, grayish surface. No great pressure should be applied, and you should strive to produce an even effect. You will need to use some care on the edges and points (if there are any, as in the case of Chippendale trays) to prevent breaking through the varnish and paint. After carefully wiping away the tiny slivers of steel wool and other dust with a tack pad, you are ready for the second coat. These directions are followed for five coats.

The sixth coat of varnish must be Valspar. If it is heated, two coats may be needed, but if it is put on at room temperature (about 70 degrees), perhaps one coat will do. With two coats, the steel-wool treatment should be applied after each coat. In the case of a second coat, the steel-wool treatment is followed by one with No. 600 wet sandpaper, a special paper used with water as a lubricant. Although this paper is extremely fine, it cuts very rapidly and only moderate pressure should be used. We simply give the tray a light once-over with this, after which the tray is rinsed in clean water to remove the grit.

RUBBING DOWN

Rubbing down is continued in the style used by cabinetmakers. First a mixture of crude oil (drugstores have it) and pumice is used. The crude oil (say a soup-spoonful) is placed on the tray, and a few pinches of pumice are thrown on it. We do not seek a thick paste but rather a semiliquid mixture. The thicker the pumice-oil mixture, the faster the pumice will cut (pumice is a mild abrasive), and pumice can cut far too fast at times, especially on edges. The pumice-oil mixture is moved about with a pad of clean cheesecloth and with only moderate pressure. Uniform treatment should be attempted. Perhaps the rubbing should not be continued for more than a half hour.

After the pumice has been used for the required time, it is wiped away and the same operation is repeated, this time with a mixture of crude oil and rotten stone, which is a much finer abrasive than pumice. Here, too, the rubbing is continued for about a half hour. In all cases, of course, both sides of trays are treated equally in the use of steel wool, pumice, and rotten stone.

After the rubbing down with rotten stone, the excess material is wiped away with a clean cloth, and the tray is washed in clean warm water to which has been added mild soap chips, such as Ivory. A gentle washing is followed by complete rinsing in plenty of clean warm water, after which the tray is allowed to dry.

FINAL ANTIQUING

This operation can complete the job unless you wish to antique your tray. Antiquing is not too difficult. It consists of placing a transparent but off-color (on the brown side) covering over the entire tray. To get the antique effect, use Valspar varnish to which has been added a small amount of burnt umber. Before the umber is placed in the varnish, a small amount of varnish (just about enough to cover the tray once) is poured into a clean saucer. The burnt umber is squeezed from the tube into the varnish and mixed, a little at a time, until you feel that you have the right color. It should be kept in mind that from three to five coats of this colored varnish are to be put on and that the first coat—or any coat, for that matter—should not be too dark. Darkness builds up as the coats are applied. There need be little treatment with steel wool between the successive coats. Of course, if you find, because of lack of experience, that the first coat produces a sufficiently dark effect, you should not make further applications. No harm will be done, although it is advisable to build up these last antiquing coats to produce a long-wearing surface that will last for many years.

The last application of the antique varnish-color mixture may be followed by a short treatment with steel wool, pumice, and rotten stone. The final result will be a thing of satisfying beauty.

Inasmuch as there are several widely known ways in which the antique effect may be achieved and heaven only knows how many private ways not generally known, you may at times want to try your hand at a method other than the one described above. In that case, you may take a fling at the following directions:

The process of antiquing is begun with an application of clear Valspar, which is given 48 hours to dry. Then a bit of raw or burnt umber (or Vandyke brown, if you wish) is mixed with a bit of turpentine to a little less than cream consistency. This is applied in a thin, even coat over the whole tray with a good brush and is then permitted to stand for a few hours to become partially dry. By this time most of the turpentine will have evaporated, but the remainder of the mixture will still be in a workable state. At this time several thicknesses of clean cheesecloth are wrapped around the index finger, and this pad is used to wipe away excess material and to create highlights, shading, etc. If this is done with a good eye, the result can be very pleasing. Should it meet with your complete satisfaction, put the tray aside for 48 hours until the toning and antiquing have had time to set up hard. After this, apply several coats of clear Valspar, with the rubbing process after each one.

CHAPTER X

Decorated Tinware

Toward the end of the eighteenth century, sheet metal commonly known as "tin" began to be imported into the metal-starved states of the American Union. As manufactured in Scotland (from which part of the British Empire came most of the early imports to America), hot sheet iron was immersed in baths of molten tin, and when it came forth it was coated with a thin film of the latter metal. Not only did the tin produce an anticorrosion surface but it provided a surface that could be soldered. Soldering meant easy fabrication.

It was natural that this tin-coated sheet iron should be seized upon for making certain utensils. There were few potteries in America at that time, and the better grades of pewter were quite beyond the means of the poor provincials. Consequently, when Yankee peddlers started to appear with tin trays, cashboxes, coffee-pots, tea canisters, candleholders, and breadbaskets, they found a ready sale. These things sold still faster when their New England manufacturers (especially in the vicinity of Berlin, Connecticut) began to decorate the various pieces first with stencils and then with freehand painted designs. Such ware was said to have been "japanned," a term still used and one that harks back to a finish that began in the Orient. Japanned ware, so far as America was concerned, involved dark or black backgrounds painted on tin, over which were placed the stenciled or hand-painted designs. Eventually, articles so produced were referred to as "tinware."

Tinware began to be produced on a large scale in New England in the early 1820s, and the Yankee cart peddlers lugged many thousands of pieces of it out of Massachusetts and Connecticut—so much, indeed, that some states soon decreed that each peddler had to license himself before he would be permitted to distribute his wares. So crippling were the license fees in some instances that a profitable trade could no longer be carried on through the agency of the peddler, and some of the more prosperous producers of tole or tinware set up factories in the states that had made it so embarrassing for the cartmen. Soon the industry was established in Pennsylvania, New York, and New Jersey.

This ware was produced almost continuously between the years 1810 and 1890, although during the last years of the nineteenth century no effort was made to decorate anything but trays and tea or coffee canisters. After all, the decorated teapot or coffeepot was not exactly practical.

Before we take up the subject of decorating tin plate, as it is called now, we should say a word or two about sources of supply for fabricated articles ready to paint. New trays in old-style shapes may be obtained in a number of sizes from any well-stocked art-supply house. Other articles are not so supplied. To obtain candle-holders, tea canisters, cashboxes, coffeepots, etc., we shall have to search for old pieces needing redecoration. Inasmuch as millions of pieces of tole ware were produced and sold over a long period —for most of the nineteenth century—a great quantity of such work still remains. Rare, indeed, are the antique shops that do not offer a piece or two in unredecorated form, and the same holds for auctions at old farmhouses. Farm attics still yield tinware that was put away by grandmothers many years ago when American pottery first began to replace pewter (in the 1830s) and later tole ware.

When unredecorated pieces of tole ware are available, they do not usually cost a great deal. A dollar or two will purchase almost anything. Tin candleholders, of which countless thousands were produced between 1830 and 1870, may sell for as little as twenty-five cents.

Of course, if you are clever mechanically, and can solder with ease, there is no reason why you cannot make a number of these

articles yourself, either from sheet-tin plate to be obtained from a
local heating-supply shop or by making use of tin cans, which can
easily be converted into coffee canisters and other items. Figure 44
shows some of the articles that were made during the early days of
the tole-ware industry and their shapes.

In Chapter IX, dealing with hand-painted trays, we learned
how to prepare tinware for painting. It will be recalled that great
emphasis was placed on the need for clean metal surfaces before
undercoatings are put on. Those instructions apply to the stripping
of old tole ware; we must make sure that the metal is scrupulously
clean, that we refrain from even touching it with our fingers after
it has been cleaned.

Fig. 44. Some of the simple utensil tinware forms
employed in the years between 1820 and 1860.

BACKGROUND COLOR

Over the years the background colors used on tole ware varied a great deal, with black and deep brown used extensively in the early part of the nineteenth century. Later, dark greens were used and sometimes deep reds. Buff and yellow were also employed, especially on toilet sets and coal hods, both of these being products of the second half of the nineteenth century. The choice of background color depended upon the nature of the article and the kind of decoration. For instance, very light colors were usually avoided on serving trays because they showed stains too easily.

Here the hobbyist may follow the instructions in Chapter IX for undercoatings and background painting, but the following variations may also be used. Some workers, in choosing black for a background, use asphalt paint, which is inexpensive and durable if of the right quality. A brand called Masury will set up hard and durable within a few hours.

Asphalt paint is flowed on rather than painted on, the idea being to eliminate as many brush strokes as possible. To help achieve smoothness, the softest camel's-hair brushes should be used. Still another means of obtaining a smooth finish is to warm the asphalt paint gently in a pan of hot water before it is applied. We place the can or jar in water and bring the temperature to about 130 degrees. Because this makes the paint extremely liquid, giving it a tendency to weep, we try to avoid painting on perpendicular surfaces. We also try not to overload the brush, simply dipping it in the paint and carrying it away just short of the dripping point.

The jet-black asphalt paint can be easily changed to varying degrees of brown by dilution with turpentine and varnish or turpentine alone. For instance, deep, rich brown may be obtained by mixing 2 parts of asphalt paint with 1 part of varnish and 1 part of turpentine. A light, golden tint results from mixing 1 part of asphalt paint with 1 part of turpentine.

If, after using asphalt paint, you are not satisfied, you can remove the coating easily, before it dries, with a rag generously moistened with turpentine.

No matter what the material used for backgrounds, it is always advisable to put a coat or two of Valspar varnish over it. Asphalt paint is no exception. Here the directions in Chapter IX should be followed. Of course, an especially good varnished surface should always be established on serving trays; no other article of decorated tinware requires such painstaking attention.

Any good-quality black enamel or flat black paint can be used for tinware backgrounds. Many experienced workers prefer flat black, which provides a surface texture similar to an egg shell. Repeated coverings of varnish after the designs have been painted or stenciled leave no evidence that flat black has been employed.

Again care must be taken in applying the paint; too heavy a coat will tend to weep, or gather in drops. With trays and other flat articles, weeping may be prevented by painting them in a flat (horizontal) position. Painting a tea canister or a coffeepot is more difficult; but you can avoid trouble if you are patient enough to thin the paint considerably and to apply two or three very thin coats, permitting each coat to dry overnight before the next one is applied.

USE OF SPRAY

Of course, the ideal way to apply very thin paint—and it *must* be thin for this method—is by spraying. With a fine spray, an evenly deposited coat can be put on easily and quickly. Three applications of thin paint will usually be necessary to build up a suitable foundation.

The most suitable covering of all for spraying is black lacquer. The speed with which it dries prevents dust from gathering and allows the worker to put on one coat after another within an hour's time, so that a foundation may be built up in a single afternoon. Of course, applying lacquer with a brush and in its original consistency as supplied in the can is another story. Brush application of lacquer can be extremely troublesome because it must be flowed on and because it dries so quickly that the worker cannot go back over surfaces without smearing them.

If you feel that the lacquer surface is a little too glossy to suit your fancy or to take your japan or oil colors, you can treat the surface with fine steel wool and then wipe the dust away with a rag moistened in turpentine, which will not dissolve the lacquer.

If lacquer is used, there is no reason why a finishing coat of varnish cannot be put on after the designs have been painted. The worker is warned, however, that while varnish may be applied over lacquer, lacquer cannot be applied over anything but itself without disastrous results. The reason for this is that the powerful solvents used in lacquer are practically the same as those used in paint removers. Hence, lacquer acts to some extent like a paint remover on anything over which it is used. Of course, the same thing is true when lacquer is applied to lacquer, but since the two coats are the same material they blend perfectly with each other.

Thus far we have been discussing dark colors, but lighter colors were also used as backgrounds for certain articles of tinware. Where buff is to be used for backgrounds, a more proper color may be achieved by adding a bit of black to the paint, the black coming from a tube of japan or artist's oil colors. This gives an antique shade to the paint. I know some skilled workers who first flow the color on and then work some black into the surface with a small camel's-hair brush, using only a tiny bit at a time.

EXECUTING THE DESIGN

With backgrounds painted, we are now ready to apply our free-hand designs or stencils. The successful painting of freehand designs on tole ware (sometimes called brush-stroke painting) does not call for artistic talent beyond the scope of average skill. Actually, you will need only practice, patience, and a firm hand. A certain amount of self-confidence and a calm, peaceful mind will also help.

There is really no reason to be tense or nervous while painting designs, even though it may be your first job and you may lack the confidence that comes only with experience. After all, if you make a mess of the first few strokes of a painting, or indeed of the single-color application of a whole design, the remedy is simple enough: A clean cloth soaked with turpentine will remove the fresh paint in a jiffy, and you can start all over again. You simply work at it until your achievement satisfies you. And don't forget that you can always practice and gain experience by painting tin cans before embarking on a real project.

MOTIFS

Before you begin to paint tole ware, study some genuinely old examples of such painting in books dealing with antiques and in antique shops and museums. You will note in particular that all such painting was relatively simple, involved but a few motifs, and was in fact a kind of folk art. If your studies are at all extensive, you will also note that there were two main divisions of the art, one belonging to New England and one belonging to Pennsylvania, the latter showing unmistakable signs of German influence.

Chief among the motifs used, regardless of the source of their inspiration, were such simple things as leaves, stems, flowers, fruit, etc. Among the fruits employed, the tomato (then called the

Fig. 45. Hand-painted tinware of the 1830s with the "love apple" (tomato) motif. (*Courtesy of the Society for the Preservation of New England Antiquities.*)

Fig. 46. Sample brush strokes that can be used freehand for producing suitable decorative devices on tinware.

"love apple" and not considered edible) was perhaps the most prominent. Many pieces were decorated without any particular motif, simply with well-ordered brush strokes applied in design form. Samples of such strokes are illustrated in Fig. 46.

Some artistically talented hobbyists will find that they are able to develop so many different combinations of simple brush strokes for really attractive designs that they will not have to use naturalistic motifs, such as fruit and leaves. Brush-stroke skill, however, need not be limited to talented workers. Anyone can achieve artistic effects if he or she will take time to practice brush control, for without stencils or drawings it is the brush alone that does the trick. Of course, a drawing may be used for guidance, but only so that the worker can look at it as he paints. As a matter of fact, this procedure is recommended for all free brushwork; otherwise the painting is apt to be out of proportion and badly fitted to the space it is to occupy. Few, indeed, are those who could start painting without a design and wind up with a well-proportioned, well-fitted job. It is far better for the beginner to draw or paint his design on paper first.

Let us assume that we wish to paint a tea canister that has a height of 9 inches and a circumference of 14 inches. If we cut a piece of drawing paper 9 by 14 inches, it will fit perfectly when wrapped around the outside of the canister. If we draw our design on this piece of paper, we shall then be able to judge its appropriateness in all respects. We may even want to color the drawing with water colors. At any rate, it is placed beside us as a guide in painting the tea canister.

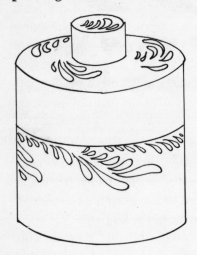

Fig. 47. Tin canister decorated solely with stripes and brush strokes.

BRUSH STROKES

Referring again to the brush strokes illustrated in Fig. 46, I highly recommend that you practice these strokes and such others as may occur to you. The practicing should be done on a surface that is just as smooth as the surface of prepared tinware, for the ease with which a brush will glide is important. Therefore, practicing should not be done on rough surfaces or on drawing paper with too much "tooth." To become reasonably proficient, you must practice many hours in a perfectly relaxed mood.

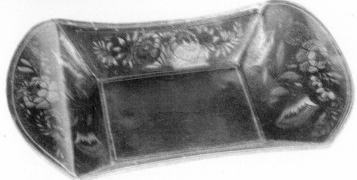

PLATE IV

Further examples of modern brush-stroke painting on tinware. (*Courtesy of Katherine Worden. Photograph by David E. Miller.*)

Downward pressure has much to do with the creation of good free-stroke work, because it spreads the brush and thus controls the width of the stroke. Most of the design elements shown in Fig. 46 are produced by the simple control of brush pressure. In one case, for example, the tip of the brush is applied first; then, as the brush begins to move, it is given sudden downward pressure, followed by a sudden lifting. The result is a pointed, leaf-like mark.

TRACING DESIGNS

For those who find, even after much practice, that they cannot control a brush properly, there is another way in which these quaint designs can be painted. This method does not produce the charm of work that is done by unguided brush strokes alone, but it is comparatively easy to do. You simply pick out a design and sketch it on a piece of paper, as noted in connection with the tea canister mentioned a few paragraphs back. You then draw the design directly on the prepared article of tinware, using a soapstone pencil. Naturally, the drawing is done in outline only, and the various elements are then filled in with paint of the correct color. The result will be a bit stiffer than work done freehand, but it may still offer a high degree of satisfaction to those who cannot accomplish the work in any other manner.

DECORATING WITH STENCILS

Stencils as well as brush-stroke designs were used on old pieces of tinware, and there is little or no difference in the technique of applying a stencil to a chair, a tray, or a tea canister.

The application of metallic powders to tinware follows the same routine as in their application to furniture and chairs. The first coat of Valspar must be at the proper stage of tackiness; the stencil must be held firmly to prevent even the slightest degree of shifting; you must watch for air-borne metallic powders, carefully wipe away excess powder before the stencil is removed, etc.

Most of the trays produced in the early part of the nineteenth century were stenciled with metallic powders practically the same as those available today in about eight shades of gold (from lemon to dark), copper, and silver (aluminum). They are applied exactly as in the case of furniture—with a chamois or a piece of velvet over the index finger, which is dipped in the powder, carried to the stencil, and pressed into the tacky varnish with a slight twist, which helps to polish the deposit.

BORDERS FOR TRAYS

The motifs used on utensils were often quite different from those used on furniture. For example, borders were rarely used on furniture, the exceptions being clock glasses, chair slats, and mirrors, although many utensils, whether hand-painted or stenciled, had border decorations. This was especially true of trays, and in Fig. 48, we see typical border decorations so employed. Also, many stenciled trays bore actual scenes in the center—young love during courtship, buildings, a locomotive and cars, etc. A really wide range of pictorial material was employed, at times involving human beings, animals, and birds. At other times just a modest and ordinary floral, leaf, and bird design was used, as illustrated in Fig. 49.

When it comes to finding and copying stenciled designs for trays and other tinware articles, no energetic worker should feel at a loss. There are many sources for good authentic designs, many of them in places where they may be copied from original articles.

Fig. 48. Brush-applied suggestions for the decoration of borders on trays, etc.

Fig. 49.   Bird, fountain, floral design suitable for the center of a tray. Beginners might well try a simple design such as this that can be painted in freehand. It may be done in gold.

The copying is done on tracing cloth or paper, as described in Chapter III. Many antique shops have such originals, and a courteous request may easily bring the invitation to "help yourself." An hour's careful tracing in a good light or near a window may supply us with several new and original designs for our collection.

But what if the design is too small or too large for the tray or other article we have, although our article is the same shape as the one from which our design is being copied? Here is an idea we might use: Regardless of the difference in size of the piece of tinware, we copy the design in India ink. If the design is too small, we photograph it and have an enlargement made to the exact size we need for the tray upon which the design is to be used. Or we can have a photostat of our drawing made in any size we wish. Tracing cloth is then placed over the photographic or photostatic print, and the design is retraced.

The same procedure, in reverse, is used if the design needs to be reduced in size, although this will be necessary only for very small articles.

PAINTING STRIPES

The painting of stripes is looked upon by many beginners as the most difficult job of all. Yet all tea canisters—indeed, all round articles of any kind—always had stripes, and if we are to make our work authentic, we must put them in. There can be no wavering of the hand; it must move along in a perfect plane if the stripe is to be straight and true. If the brush wavers sideways, the stripe will be wavy; if the brush pressure varies, the line will vary greatly in width. The little turntable and the brush support shown in Fig. 50 will be found very useful in installing stripes that appear as if they had been painted by a professional. Also, in painting the edge of a tray (see Fig. 33), striping can be much easier because the guide will at least eliminate wavy motion.

Striping may be done with very small camel's-hair brushes, but it is best done with a quill striping brush, the hairs of which may be 2 inches long. Naturally, a striping brush should carry as much paint as possible, because every time a line is interrupted and started again, owing to the need to reload the brush, it is difficult not to show the break in continuity.

This does not mean, however, that we should load a brush with so much paint that it will drip all the way to our work. The excess should be gently scraped off on the edge of the container before the brush is brought into use. The brush is always held between the thumb and first two fingers.

Where black backgrounds were used, yellow was a highly favored striping color in the old days, and it still offers the sort of contrast that is pleasant as well as authentic. Red was also used considerably on black backgrounds. Buff or other light backgrounds called for such striping colors as deep red, brown, or black.

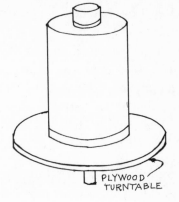

Fig. 50. Aided by a simple turntable, the placing of stripes on cylindrical tinware articles is made very easy. A support may be used to hold the brush at a certain level.

MIXING PAINT FOR STRIPING

Special paint mixtures involving either japan or oil colors are used in painting in stripes. Inasmuch as these mixtures do not come already prepared, each worker will have to make his own in the following manner: To 1 teaspoonful of clear varnish (either 24- or 4-hour) add 1 teaspoonful of turpentine. Color from a tube is added to this mixture until a creamlike consistency is reached.

The yellow used for striping on black surfaces is prepared by mixing 1 part of chrome yellow, 1 part of Vandyke brown, and 1 part of yellow ocher. This combination of colors is mixed with the turpentine-varnish combination referred to above.

Oftentimes two stripes were placed on the edge of a tray, one relatively wide and one very narrow, with a small separation (⅜ inch or so) between the two. The narrow stripe was little more than a hairline. The wide stripe might have been light green, and the narrow one a brilliant yellow, a very pleasing combination on a dark background. An excellent green for this purpose may be mixed by taking chrome green and adding a bit of lampblack and raw umber to it. In painting a double stripe, it is always advisable to permit the first one to dry before the second one is painted. This will prevent smudging.

When installing bronze or gold stripes, some workers simply paint in a stripe of clear varnish and press bronze powder into it after it has reached the tacky stage.

Thanks to a new product on the market, striping not only on trays but on clock glasses, mirrors, and other articles may be done in 23-carat gold. Even the complete home regilding of old picture frames, long the wish of those who deal with antiques, is now possible at very little expense.

The new product, called Golden Touch and manufactured by M. Swift and Sons, of Hartford, Connecticut, is simply a decalcomania-transfer sheet covered with 23-carat gold leaf. A mere soaking in water and subsequent application to any surface will deposit the gold leaf, thus avoiding the professional method of lifting gold leaf from a book with a gilder's tip, which demands a great deal of skill. In using Golden Touch for striping, you simply cut a strip the correct width from a sheet and transfer the gold to the edge of the tray.

CHAPTER XI

Painting on Glass

THOSE WHO WISH to perfect themselves in the kind of art used to decorate furniture 125 years ago will eventually come upon the problem of painting in reverse on glass. Such art is pictorial although often combined with stenciling.

In the early nineteenth century, reverse painting on glass was employed on the lower sections of the glass doors of shelf clocks and on the upper sections of small wall mirrors. Owing to the ravages of time and breakage, it is unusual to find these paintings in a state of good preservation. Most of them have been badly scratched and nicked, and the paint has often peeled to such an extent that the picture is almost wholly destroyed.

The best examples of good clock-glass painting were produced between 1815 and 1835, and many of them came from the Plymouth, Connecticut, factory of Eli Terry and his sons. His famous pillar-and-scroll clock case was so decorated, the glass having not only an exquisitely executed scene but a beautiful stenciled border as well. Some idea of the amount of money a worker might save in painting his own clock glass may be obtained from prices quoted by professional artist-restorers: twenty-five to forty dollars for clock glasses and in the neighborhood of twenty dollars for mirrors.

Even the worker with only modest skill need not hesitate to try his hand at this work. No great artistic talent is required, since all such paintings were primitive in nature, especially the pastoral and sea scenes. No doubt the people who painted them on a mass-production basis in the old clock factories had no more artistic skill than you or I. After all, such paintings had to be produced

109

Fig. 51. Close-up of stenciled border on Terry clock glass (1825) and stenciled pilaster on the same clock. Both are original in every respect.

quickly. Therefore, all artistic subtleties were avoided and solid colors were much used. The paintings, although gaudy and stiff, nevertheless have a quaint charm. We can say in truth that a painting on a clock or mirror glass can easily be too good—so good, in fact, as to be out of place and out of period.

In later years, beginning in the 1840s, the paintings on clock glasses began to deteriorate and those on mirror glasses practically disappeared. Much less time was spent in such painting, with less detail and certainly with far less charm. Whereas the paintings on all the earlier clocks were surrounded with a neatly stenciled

Fig. 52. An original clock glass painted in the late 1840s.

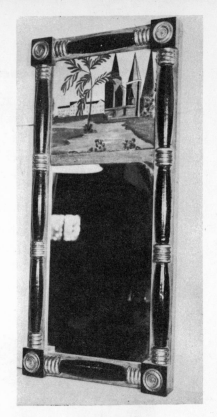

Fig. 53. A mirror of the later American Empire period (1821) with painted glass panel.

Fig. 54. Two Federal period (circa 1790) American mirrors with hand-painted top panels.

border 1 to 1½ inches wide, the clockmakers of the 1840s had no time to bother with such decoration. Therefore, those who would restore the paintings of old clocks should make sure they are not installing an early clock scene with a border on a clock case of the 1840s or 1850s.

MAKING STENCIL BORDERS

Before you do any painting on an old clock glass, it is wise to put on the stenciled border design, which should be a rather complicated one. Figure 55 illustrates the type of stencil used on a Terry clock as of 1825. You will notice that it fills the space, with little blank space left.

Fig. 55. The full glass painting of a Terry wooden-works shelf clock made in 1825, still in an un-retouched condition.

The stencil design is cut on a piece of stencil paper the size of the bottom glass in the clock and is held in place with Scotch tape. Before this is done, however, a decision will have to be made as to the method by which the gold is to be applied—whether we are to use the same system we used in applying stencils to furniture with bronze powders or whether we are to use fine gold leaf. Naturally, we cannot use gold leaf if we plan to shade or bleed off any part of the stenciled design. No shading was used on the border stenciling of old clocks, however, so the choice between powder and gold leaf introduces no artistic problem.

If you are going to use powder, the procedure is practically the same as that employed in applying stencil designs to furniture. You must bear in mind, however, that none of the volatile ingredients of the varnish is absorbed by the glass, and therefore you may have to wait a bit longer for the varnish to set up to the desired tacky stage than you do when you apply it to wood. Instead of the 24-hour varnish, it may be wise to use Super-Valspar, which needs only a few hours to become tacky. When this stage is reached, the gold powder is put in solid. A light-gold shade is most desirable for such work.

If you wish to use gold leaf for your stencils, it is best to substitute regular gold size for the varnish. You can purchase this size ready to apply, or you can make it yourself in accordance with the directions given later. In no case should even the most dilute varnish be used as a size for gold leaf.

Gold leaf comes by the book and the pack, a book holding twenty-five leaves and a pack being made up of twenty books, or 500 leaves. Each sheet measures 3⅜ inches square, and usually a small job will require a book or less. In short, a book will cover a surface approximately 1½ feet square. A pack will cover 30 square feet. Gold leaf may be purchased from any large paint house, or the local sign painter may be willing to sell a book or two or to tell you where he obtains his supply. Golden Touch leaf may also be used.

Leaf is made in a number of different colors and with different degrees of purity, some being better than 23-carat gold. This high purity gives protection against tarnish over a long period of time. The high-purity forms are usually referred to as "deep," since they have the real color of gold. Lemon-color gold, an alloy mixture more yellow in tone, is 18½-carat and is often used on glass. Pale gold (16½-carat) is still lighter.

Silver sheet may also be obtained, twenty-five leaves to the book, 3¼ inches square.

Before you start gilding on glass, the surface must be rendered scrupulously clean. After washing it with soap and water, you go over the glass with whiting and water and then with alcohol and tissue paper. *Clean* is the word!

Next you prepare the water size used as the adhesive for the leaf. Naturally, with so fine a covering as gold leaf, a very light adhesive or size is required; otherwise the gold leaf would not be smooth. The size is so easy to prepare that there is little reason why you should go to the expense of purchasing the ready-to-use preparations.

A good size for glass is made from distilled water and three No. 00 gelatin capsules, both of which may be purchased at any drugstore. A pint of distilled water is brought to a boil, and the separated capsules are placed in it and allowed to dissolve. Then another pint of distilled water is added. This solution is strained through blotting paper or cheesecloth and is placed in a sterilized bottle.

Some workers prefer a size prepared with fish glue or Russian isinglass. With either material, a piece about the size of a quarter is used instead of the gelatin capsules. The procedure is the same.

The size is applied to the part of the glass that is to be gilded with a clean, dust-free brush. As you proceed with the gilding, you must be sure that the still-ungilded portions of the design are kept constantly wet by repeated applications of size until they are covered with leaf. *Therefore, you should not attempt to cover too large a space at a time.*

It is best to start applying the gold at the upper left-hand corner and to work across the top so that if the size runs down it will not run onto gilded surfaces. This precaution is taken if the glass is vertical, though it is better to work on a horizontal surface if possible.

The gold leaf is handled in the following manner: First, cut a heavy piece of cardboard the size of the book of gold leaf. This is for backing and is held underneath the book.

Now the first sheet of paper (the gold leaf is sandwiched between sheets of special paper) is folded back halfway to expose the gold beneath it. This folded sheet is then used as a guide to cut the gold leaf in half by running your fingernail across it very lightly. We use only half a sheet at a time, for a whole sheet is too heavy and far too difficult to handle.

Having been cut, the half sheet of gold leaf is ready to be lifted to the sized surface. To do this it is necessary to use a gilder's tip, since the sheets of gold are so thin that it would be impossible to handle them with the fingers. The gilder's tip is a fine brush made of badger's hair. In order to pick up the leaf, you electrify the brush by gently brushing it over your hair. A single pass is enough to electrify it so that when it is touched to the gold leaf, the leaf will adhere to the brush and can be carried to the sized surface. The half sheet is carefully laid on the wet surface, and then the gilder's tip is used to brush it out flat.

Here you must be careful not to allow the hairs of the gilder's tip to touch the wet surface. If they do, a tiny amount of grease or hair oil will be deposited on the size and will cause a water break; the size will separate and bare the glass beneath. If gold leaf is placed over such an open section in the wet surface, the leaf will soon peel at that point.

The leaf is applied until the entire design is covered, the worker being careful not to waste too much gold leaf by going too far over the edges of the area being covered. The overlap between sheets should be, so far as possible, not more than ⅛ inch.

The gold leaf in place, you must wait for the whole thing to dry completely, after which you must go around the edge of the design and scrape off the excess gold leaf beyond the borders. Burnishing is then in order. This is done with a clean piece of absorbent cotton or velvet, which is rubbed briskly but gently over the back of the gold. Burnishing invariably opens up holes and reveals other imperfections in the gold, which must be patched. The gold leaf already in place is covered with size, and small pieces of leaf are applied to the spots needing attention. After this is dry, the whole thing is burnished again.

Then the gold is washed with clean water at the boiling point, the water being applied with the sort of absorbent cotton used in hospitals. Such treatment adds greatly to the brilliance of the gold.

The design is now ready to be backed up with a paint that must dry very hard. Lampblack ground in japan is a good backing-up preparation. Colored lacquers may also be used as a backing. These may be further covered with spar varnish.

PAINTING SCENERY ON GLASS

After the stenciled border has been put in place by whatever method, you are ready to proceed with the painting of the scenery. The first step is to find a proper subject or scene, which, if you are not especially skilled in drawing human figures or animals, may take the form illustrated in Fig. 56. Whatever scene you choose, whether it is original or copied, you first draw it with pencil or India ink on a piece of paper exactly the size of the empty space within the stenciled border of the clock glass. Therefore, the scene drawn on the paper should be exactly that which you wish to transfer to the glass. Transferring the drawing to glass, however, would be a nuisance. Therefore, you fasten the drawing you made on paper to the *front* of the clock glass with adhesive tape so that the drawing will show through to the back of the glass or the surface upon which the painting is to be made.

You must bear in mind at all times in this work that everything is done in reverse. This is especially important in painting the scenery. For instance, in ordinary work, trees may be painted over a previously painted-in background. If this were done on a glass

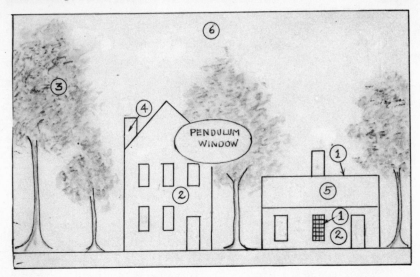

Fig. 56. A suggestion for a clock-glass sketch. Numbers indicate the sequence in which the various parts are to be painted. Building outlines (*1*) can be ruled in first with India ink.

picture, however, the trees would not be seen; the blue of the sky would cover them up when the scene was viewed from the right side. Hence, trees that come up into the sky are painted first, and then the sky is painted around them. This sequence must be watched very carefully throughout the whole job.

One way to keep out of trouble in this tricky and confusing business is to study the drawing and mark each space *1, 2, 3,* etc., as in Fig. 56, so that the sequence figure is before you at all times.

It will be obvious, of course, that you should be careful about painting in adjacent areas or second surfaces before the paint or enamel over which you will be working is perfectly dry.

The ordinary enamels that come in small cans and loud colors may be used for this work. Colors may be changed by mixing the various shades. Some workers prefer tube oil colors mixed with a bit of turpentine, though these may require as long as a week to dry. My choice is the japan colors mixed with varnish because of the shorter drying period.

CHAPTER XII

Painting Clockfaces

THOUSANDS OF CLOCKS were made for the mass market between the years 1820 and 1860, and a great many of them are still around, some rendering yeoman service and some stored away in attics as family heirlooms with the hope that one day some member of the family will haul them down and restore them. Chances are that some of the original paint has scaled off the glass, if the glass is not completely broken, and that the clockface is in need of considerable repair. Such repair may involve retouching the painted surface or supplying a completely new paint job, including numerals, which may be either Arabic or Roman, both having been used throughout the whole history of American clockmaking.

While many of the clockfaces for both shelf and tall clocks were made of painted and engraved brass from the seventeenth century onward, the men who started the wooden-works clock industry in Connecticut during the first twenty-five years of the nineteenth century (Eli Terry, Chauncey Jerome, Riley Whiting, etc.) made all their clockfaces from carefully seasoned wood about ⅜ inch thick. To prevent warping of these thin panels, two cleats about ⅜ inch square were nailed to their backs.

WOODEN FACE PANELS

Those who would restore old clocks may be faced with the problem of making a new face if the old one has been lost or has become so badly warped and split as to be beyond repair. If such is the case, it may be difficult to find a piece of ⅜-inch wood without knots measuring at least 10 by 10 inches. Ordinary plywood must be ruled out because of the grain, although some of the

118

more expensive plywoods such as gum or mahogany are suitable for this purpose. There is also a form of Masonite sheet, sold as "underlayment," which, given a coat of shellac and two coats of flat white, will be suitable for the application of old-ivory or plain-white paint. All old faces were either white or ivory.

Each coat of flat white should be sanded down with No. 00 sandpaper before the enamel is put on. Two thin coats of white or ivory enamel should be applied, with sanding in between, rather than one heavy coat. The second coat is brushed gently with fine steel wool to cut its high gloss and to provide a better surface for drawing in the numbers.

LAYING OUT THE FACE

The initial operation in making the face layout is to find the exact center of the blank clockface surface. This is easily done by placing a yardstick from corner to corner and marking the point at which the two lines cross. A compass point is then placed on this point, and the outermost circle is drawn in with a soft pencil. On the ordinary shelf clocks of the 1820s and 1830s, this outer circle was usually about 10 inches in diameter, while the inner one was about 8 inches in diameter. The numerals, whether Arabic or Roman, are drawn or painted between these lines. It will be advisable to sketch the numerals with a soft pencil to make sure that the arrangement is satisfactory before the painting is done.

However, before the numerals are sketched in, it will be necessary to divide the circle on the clockface into 12 equal parts, as illustrated in Fig. 57. Inasmuch as 12 can be divided equally into 360 degrees, this is no problem; with a small protractor the divisions are marked off at every 30 degrees. At the points where these lines intersect the circles, light pencil marks should be made. These lines represent the center marks for the numbers that are to be sketched in with a soft pencil. In drawing the Arabic numeral 12, the 1 will be placed on one side of the middle line and the 2 on the other side. If the Roman numeral XII is used, the center line will divide the X and the two II's. For single Arabic or Roman

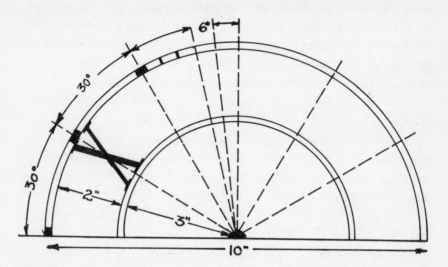

Fig. 57. How a clockface is laid out after the basic coat of ivory or white is laid.

Fig. 58. Painting in Arabic clockface numerals with a small brush and India ink.

numerals, the center line runs through the center of each number.

The circle comprising the clock dial must also be divided into 60 parts or minutes. This, too, is very easily accomplished with a protractor, the minute marks being 6 degrees apart. These marks are later drawn in with a ruling pen filled with India ink.

PAINTING THE NUMERALS

When the complete clockface is laid out, any one of several mediums may be used to paint in the numbers, circles, and minute marks. India ink is excellent, except for the fact that mistakes or slips made with it are not easily eradicated. If this is used, it will be best to outline the numerals with a heavy-line pen and then fill them in with a small brush.

Flat black, well thinned with turpentine, may also be used for painting numerals. The advantage here is that if we make a slip with a brush, the whole number may be wiped away with a cloth soaked in turpentine, and we can start over again.

In any event, it is best to draw the two circles with the aid of a compass and India ink, regardless of the type of paint used for the numerals.

Some of the old wooden-works clockfaces were rather heavily ornamented. Almost without exception, they had spandrels painted in bronze or gold in each of the four corners. These were done in relief to simulate the cast-bronze spandrels that were so widely used on tall clocks between 1650 and 1800. The relief effect was achieved by painting in the spandrel with thinned-out gesso and then, after the gesso had set up, going over it with gold or bronze. We can produce the same result (although this is not truly a gesso mixture) with a thin mixture of plaster of Paris to which considerable hide glue or fish glue has been added. Before this is applied with a small brush, we draw in the outline of the spandrels in each corner of the clockface. Typical spandrel forms are illustrated in Fig. 59.

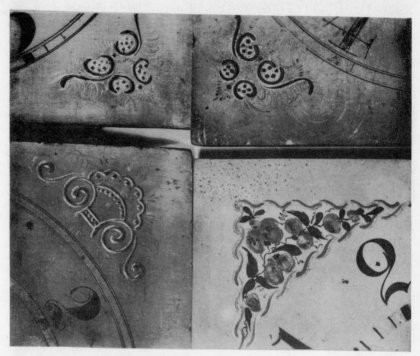

Fig. 59. Examples of painted and embossed spandrels, the latter being built up with thin gesso, after which they were gilded or painted black or red.

SPANDRELS

Not all spandrels, however, were first outlined in gesso and then painted. Many were the clockfaces produced without the gesso but with spandréls painted in with gold or other colors, sometimes with black. Nor was the use of gesso limited to spandrel-type decorations. Sometimes ornamental wreath effects were produced with gesso between the center of the clock dial and the inner circle of the space in which the numerals were painted. These gesso-produced wreaths were covered with bronze or gold.

Sometimes we find old clockfaces with wreath effects simply

painted with gold or bronze, without gesso. The decorative effects of many old clockfaces were simply painted in flat color or gold. Naturally, the relief effect was more costly to produce, and some clockmakers were satisfied to leave it out.

Occasionally we come across genuine old clockfaces that have decorative flowers or fruit with leaves painted between the numerals, the motif being repeated twelve times. In addition, we also find the spandrels and wreath between the inner circle and the center of the dial. Apparently an effort was made to fill every empty space, but the effect is too gaudy and too overdone for most taste. The careful modern restorer and painter of clockfaces will leave plenty of white space on the dials he finishes.

It will be seen in Figs. 61 and 62 that tall- or grandfather-clock faces are not shaped exactly like the faces on shelf clocks. They

Fig. 60. (Top) **Stenciled** spandrels on the clock glass of an 1850 timepiece. The background is black. *(Bottom)* The hand-painted clockface of a Terry wooden-works clock made in the 1820s. Note the hand-painted basket of flowers below the center.

Fig. 61. (*Above right*) The face of a Seth Thomas clock made (by permission of Eli Terry who invented the works and designed the case) in the early 1820s. (*Above left*) A worn painted wooden face of a tall clock (grandfather's) made by Silas Hoadley at Plymouth, Conn., about 1822.

Fig. 62. A hand-painted wooden face of a Riley Whiting woodenworks tall clock made at Winchester, Conn., about 1825.

are approximately the same size, but they have a semicircular section at the top in which invariably a scene was painted. We are talking now only about the inexpensive wooden-works clocks produced in the 1820s and 1830s. Large numbers of works intended for tall clocks were produced in those years, especially by Riley Whiting and Silas Hoadley, of Connecticut, and were carried far and wide by Yankee peddlers. Tall clocks differ from shelf clocks also in the fact that they boasted a second hand and usually a calendar hand.

Although old clockfaces were not so treated, it may be advisable for us to place an antique varnish over completed jobs, especially if the background paint is white instead of antique ivory. Before we do this, however, it will be well to paint several scrap pieces of the composition board or plywood from which the clockface was cut so that we may use them as experimental panels in achieving the right mixture of burnt umber and varnish. Ideas about depth of color vary, but if we have several small test panels, we can decide easily how much umber to add to clear varnish for the effect we wish to achieve.

Antique varnish, of course, will dry out far too glossy for the effect we desire. Hence, after it has set up hard, we go over the varnished surface with fine steel wool to cut away the last vestige of gloss. The resulting dead and grayish effect can be very easily eliminated by wiping the face with a clean cloth moistened with turpentine and then applying furniture wax. This will produce just the sort of mild, satinlike gloss that we desire.

CHAPTER XIII

Fraktur

THE PENNSYLVANIA GERMANS who settled Bucks and Lancaster counties brought with them certain folk arts and skills the most interesting of which is a decorative process referred to as "Fraktur." When properly executed, Fraktur has a quaint charm and, even more in its favor, it may be done with a great deal of originality if the worker will study even briefly the motifs used by the early practitioners of this art.

We do not need to search very far for the original inspiration that resulted in Fraktur painting. Such work was being done long before the Bavarian Germans sought William Penn's hospitality in the New World. It is quite obvious that the art evolved from the illumination of manuscripts as practiced by the monks of the Middle Ages. An examination of specimens of such manuscripts in German museums reveals how similar in schematic arrangement, color, and motifs they are to the eighteenth-century work done by the Germans in this country. As a matter of fact, such art was so solidly established as a part of the culture of the Pennsylvania Germans that it was taught in the schools well into the 1840s.

Fraktur had a wide range of uses among the Germans; it was used to illuminate psalm books, marriage certificates, bibles, baptismal papers, songs, death registers, etc. It also served as pure decoration when it was produced on parchment or paper, framed and hung on the otherwise bare walls of the German farmsteads.

The few kits used in Fraktur painting that have come to light in Pennsylvania show that the work was accomplished with very simple materials. A few water colors of narrow spectral range, a few homemade paintbrushes, as often as not bearing tufts of

126

Fig. 63. A Pennsylvania Dutch dower chest of the second half of the eighteenth century. (*Courtesy of the Metropolitan Museum of Art.*)

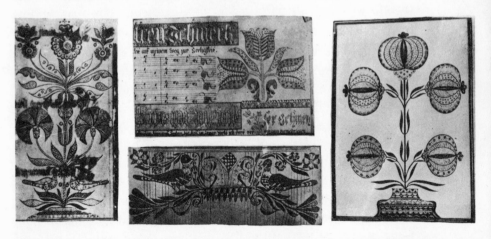

Fig. 64. Examples of gay Fraktur as practiced by the Pennsylvania Dutch. This form of decoration was not abandoned by them until the 1850s. (*Courtesy of the Pennsylvania Historical Society.*)

pussy's hair, a small supply of quill pens, and some ink completed the list of materials.

The old workers in Fraktur were all of them neophytes; none of this work, no matter how old, shows any basic artistic ability. It is all crude and primitive, and if it were not so, it would not be Fraktur.

First the early practitioners of Fraktur drew their designs in clear outline upon whatever was being decorated. This was done in ink with a quill pen. After the design was drawn, the spaces within the design were filled in with whatever colors the worker wished or with whatever colors he had at his disposal—and the supply was usually very modest. Certainly the handed-down examples of Fraktur demonstrate no subtlety in color, no shading, etc. They are simply fine outlines of the various motifs arranged in design form and filled in with water color.

If the modern worker wishes to reproduce such designs, he may use a moderately fine steel pen and some of the modern antique-brown writing ink. This ink, after exposure to summer sunlight after the color has been installed, will produce a very satisfactory antique appearance. Indeed, if the worker has taken the precaution to produce his painting on an old piece of rag paper torn from the flyleaves of an 1820 or 1830 book, he could produce something that might give an expert in antiques a considerable headache if he had to rule on its antiquity.

The motifs used by the Germans in their Fraktur work were limited and simple. The tulip was widely used and perhaps takes first place in popularity. Then came the heart, the dove, the angel, and leaves. Less frequently there appeared human figures, trees, houses, animals, wreaths, etc.

Of course, a great deal of the old German Fraktur work had script associated with it, especially the marriage certificates, memorials, etc. This was usually in German, although late specimens of the work from the first fifty years of the nineteenth century often appeared in English.

INDEX

A

Adam Brothers, 3
Antiquing, of stencils, 69, 71
 of trays, 82
 final, 92
Asphalt paint on tinware, 97

B

Background colors for tinware, 97
Background for tinware, 107
Backgrounds, light, 47
Bed, Empire, 6
Borders, stencil, 32
Bramah, Joseph, 1
Bronze powder, how to apply in stenciling, 53
 how to polish, 58
Brush, striping, 64
 varnish, how to clean, 51
Brush-stroke painting, on stenciled furniture, 48
 on tinware, 101
 on trays, 79, 80
Brushes, care of, 42
 cleaners for, 43
 dust in, 51
 proper types of, 42
 for stenciling, 13

C

Cannister, tin, painting, 102
Cape Cod benches, 69
Chair, Pennsylvania Dutch, 33
Chair seats, repairing, 40
Chairs, fancy, 4
 Hitchcock background colors of, 34
 repairing, 35, 38, 39
 Salem-made Sheraton, 8
 striping, 64
 stripping old paint from, 35
Chest, Connecticut dower, 33

Chest, Pennsylvania dower, 33
Chests, Empire, 6
Cleopatra's Barge, 8
Clockfaces, background paint for, 118
 brass, 118
 early, 118
 floral decorations on, 122
 gesso on, 121
 grandfather, 123
 laying out, 119
 Masonite, 119
 painting, 123
 painting numerals on, 121
 spandrels on, 121
 wooden, 118
Clock glasses, borders for, 110
 early painting of, 109
 painting scenery on, 116
 painting with japan colors, 116
Clocks, wooden-works, 125
Colors, background, for Hitchcock
  chairs, 34
 for stenciled furniture, 41
 for tinware, 97
 japan, 45
 mixing of, 15, 17
 opaque, 15
 transparent, 15, 16
 used over bronze, 17
Compote stencil motif, 62
Coombs, Richard, 11
Cracks, filling, 41
Crowninshield, George, 8
Crude oil with pumice, 72

D

Designs for tinware, sources of, 104

F

Fraktur, 126
 as decoration, 33
 design motifs in, 128

Fraktur, kits for, 126
  origin of, 126
  script in, 128
Frazee, Kenneth, 12
French curves for copying stencils, 21
Frescoed walls, 4
Furniture, painted English, 3

G

Gesso on clockfaces, 121
Glasses, clock, painting of, 110
Glue, use of, in repairing chairs, 39
Gold leaf, books of, 113
  burnishing, 116
  carat fineness of, 114
  for clock glasses, 113
  fish-glue size for, 114
  gelatin size for, 114
  handling, 113, 115
  Russian isinglass size for, 114
  sizes for, 113
Golden Touch, for striping, 108
  use of, on tinware, 108
Grandfather-clock faces, 123

H

Hitchcock, Lambert, death of, 7
Hitchcock chair, fancy, 5
  first, 7
Hitchcock chair advertisements, 9
Hitchcock factory, 9, 10
Hitchcock warrantee, 9

J

Japan colors, 45
  on clock glasses, 116
Japanned tinware, 95
Joints, chair, repairing, 35, 38

K

Kenny, Jack, 11
Knives for cutting stencils, 23

L

Lacquer on painted tinware, 99
Lacquers, how to use, 44
  spraying of, 44

Lye, for cleaning old trays, 78

M

Mahoganized finish, 3
Mahogany finish, imitation, 4
Masking tape for striping, 68
Masonite, for clockfaces, 119
  test panels, 26
  use of, 49
Mirror, Empire, 7
Mirrors, clock, 110
Motif, Dutch tulip, 33
  tomato, 100
Motifs, animal, for stencils, 31
  Empire era, for stencils, 29
  naturalistic, for stencils, 28
  on painted tinware, 100
  stencil, Federal period, 31
  shell, 29
  for tinware, 100, 104
Maudslay, Henry, 1

P

Paint, removal of, 36, 37
  materials for, 36
  from trays, 75
Paint removers, use of, on trays, 75
Paper, tracing, for copying stencils, 20
Primer, red, on trays, 83
Pumice, how to use, 72

R

Remover, varnish, application of, 37
Rocking settees, 9
Rubbing down trays, 92
Rubbing pad for pumice, 72
Rubbing with pumice, 72
Rust, elimination of, from trays, 80

S

Sandpaper, proper use of, 42
Scissors for cutting stencils, 23
Scraper for paint removal, 37
Seats, chair, repairing, 40
Shading stencils, 57
Size, fish glue, for gold leaf, 114
  gelatin, for gold leaf, 114

Size, Russian isinglass, for gold leaf, 114
Spandrels, clockface, 121–122
Spraying paint on tinware, 98
Steel wool, use of, 47
 on trays, 83, 91
Stencil, early use of, on American furniture, 3
 compote, 61
 as old decorative device, 1
Stencil borders for clock glasses, 112
Stenciling, applying bronze powders in, 53
 materials needed for, 13
 time element in, 59
 use of colored paint in, 60
Stencils, antiquing of, 69, 71
 application of, 51, 57
 background colors for, 41, 45
 cleaning old, for copying, 18
  with soap, 19
 composite, 61
 copying of, 18
  with drawing instruments, 21
  with India ink, 20
  materials for, 20
  with tracing cloth, 20
 cutting of, 21, 27
  knives for, 22
  scissors for, 23
 decorating tinware with, 103
 Empire motifs in, 29
 ready-cut, 18
 shading of, 57
 size of, 33
 test panels for, 23
Striping, with gold, 70
 with masking tape, 68
 on stenciled furniture, 64
 on tinware, 106
  mixing colors for, 107
 use of Golden Touch in, 108
 with yellow paint, 69
Stripping old paint from chairs, 35

T

Tack rag, making and using, 79
Terry, Eli, 1
 early clocks of, 110

Test panels, stencil, 23
Tinware, background colors for, 107, 97
 decoration of, with tracing paper, 103
 design of decoration for, 99
 japanned, 95
 old New England producers of, 94
 painted motifs for, 100
 sources of, for decorating, 95
 sources of old designs for, 104
 use of asphalt paint on, 97
Tomato motif for tinware, 100
Tracing cloth for copying stencils, 20
Trays, antiquing, 82, 89, 92
 applying design to, 88
 applying finishing coats to, 86
 applying varnish to, 87
 borders for, 104
 cleaning of, 78
 drying of, without dust, 85
 eliminating rust from, 80
 painting on, 74
 removing old paint from, 75
 rubbing down of, 92
 sources of, 74
 striping of, 80
 treating corrosion on, 81
 types, styles, and periods of, 75

U

Undercoatings for stenciled furniture, 45

V

Varnish, bubbles in, 51
 drying period of, 50
 for finish, 46
 how to apply with brush, 51
 on stenciling, 50
 Valentine's, for stencils, 59
Velvet, use of in applying bronze powders, 55
Vernis-Martin, 9

W

Wax, furniture, how to use, 73
 removal of, 38
Whitney, Eli, 1

Y

Yellow paint, mixing of, for striping, 70